LET
THEM
BE KIDS

LET THEM BE KIDS

Adventure, Boredom, Innocence, and Other Gifts Children Need

JESSICA SMARTT

W PUBLISHING GROUP

AN IMPRINT OF THOMAS NELSON

Published in Nashville, Tennessee, by W Publishing Group, an imprint of Thomas Nelson.

Thomas Nelson titles may be purchased in bulk for educational, business, fund-raising, or sales promotional use. For information, please e-mail SpecialMarkets@ThomasNelson.com.

Scripture quotations taken from *The Holy Bible*, New International Version®, NIV®. © 1973, 1978, 1984, 2011 by Biblica, Inc.® Used by permission of Zondervan. All rights reserved worldwide.

Any Internet addresses, phone numbers, or company or product information printed in this book are offered as a resource and are not intended in any way to be or to imply an endorsement by Thomas Nelson, nor does Thomas Nelson vouch for the existence, content, or services of these sites, phone numbers, companies, or products beyond the life of this book.

Library of Congress Cataloging-in-Publication Data

Names: Smartt, Jessica, author.
Title: Let them be kids : adventure, boredom, innocence, and other gifts children need / Jessica Smartt.
Description: [Nashville, Tennessee] : [W Publishing Group], [2020] | Summary: "Practical ideas and encouragement for moms who want to raise kids that honor their family values, make good decisions, pursue life creatively, and live with a deeply rooted faith"— Provided by publisher.
Identifiers: LCCN 2020006602 (print) | LCCN 2020006603 (ebook) | ISBN 9780785221272 (paperback) | ISBN 9780785221319 ebook)
Subjects: LCSH: Child rearing. | Parent and child. | Families.
Classification: LCC HQ769 .S5644 2020 (print) | LCC HQ769 (ebook) | DDC 649/.1—dc23
LC record available at https://lccn.loc.gov/2020006602
LC ebook record available at https://lccn.loc.gov/2020006603

20 21 22 23 24 LSC 10 9 8 7 6 5 4 3 2 1

Dad,
Ever since I can remember, you've brightened the
room with your eternal optimism and passion
for life. You are the world's best dad, a faithful
encourager, and an amazing Grampy.

Mom,
Home has always been where you are.
Thank you for bearing my many worries
and constantly pointing me to Jesus.

CONTENTS

CONTENTS

Let Them Be Kids: A Manifesto

We believe in childhood, in letting kids be little and awkward and snuggly and free. We believe in family, that we always have one another and that wherever we are is home. We believe in adventure and that the Good Life is more thrilling, more satisfying, more sidesplitting fun than the cheap imitations. We believe in imagination—in great books on rainy days, in long car trips with goofy entertainment—and that the good stuff happens after you set down your phone. We believe in blowing bubbles, building forts, chasing fireflies, and playing dress-up. We believe that boredom is often the beginning of something wonderful. We think puzzles, board games, hard work, and opening the door for someone should never go out of style. We believe being kind matters more than being cool, and developing character is more than winning. We know that innocence and purity are still worth fighting for. We believe in "I'm sorry" and "I'll always love you." It's not an easy thing to build a childhood. But in the long run? It's worth it—for all of us.

CHAPTER ONE

WHY CHILDHOOD MATTERS

When I was eleven years old, ten of us cousins reunited for a glorious week at Uncle Joe's lake house. The first afternoon we meandered unsupervised out to the dock to dip our toes in the water, when we noticed something magnificent. Off to one side was a giant piece of wood that had washed up on the rocky beach. It was huge—bigger than we were. The possibilities sprawled out before us like a game of Pick Up Sticks on the carpet, with the most obvious being that we had just discovered a ship. We didn't bother to get approval from the grown-ups (who I now realize were inside drinking their coffee and watching with amusement). Instead, we got busy preparing to launch our new boat.

First, we had to assemble provisions. We snuck a sleeve of saltine crackers and a few snack-sized boxes of raisins out of the pantry, along with juice boxes. We also needed oars. This was harder than we thought, because we had to get the right kind of sticks that were

1

strong enough to do the job but not so big that we would hit the oarsmen behind us.

Then it got sticky because we had to choose the passengers. This meant sorting the big kids from the little kids, and there were always those few in the middle who were questionable. I don't remember where the line was drawn, but I do remember that it ended in a fight and someone "accidentally" getting drenched in lake water. Last of all, our noble vessel needed a name. Only one was suggested; we agreed unanimously. *The Majestic*. She was beautiful, after all.

That was twenty-seven years ago.

When I look back at this glorious memory, it captures so many things that are wonderful about childhood: things such as freedom, risk, imagination, adventure, creativity, nature, friendship, and innocence. Was it dangerous to set sail on uncharted waters aboard discarded, rotting, and barely attached two-by-fours? You bet it was. That made it even better.

Likely you have your own similar-sounding childhood adventure. The thing is, the bits and pieces that make up a childhood are more than stories; *they form character*. Once a human being arrives at adulthood, many core values and traits are statistically unlikely to change in later life.[1] Of course, change is always possible. But here are a few things that tend to be fixed after arriving at adulthood:

1. Character traits, such as patience, kindness, integrity, self-discipline, and the ability to follow rules[2]
2. Habits, such as work ethic, technology use or misuse, and time management
3. Skills and abilities, such as intellectual curiosity, proficiency in music or foreign languages, reading aptitude, and the ability to communicate well in written or spoken word[3]

4. Presence of faith / view of God[4]
5. Sexual health, in the sense that habits and choices have already been made to affect one's lifelong sexual behavior and happiness[5]
6. Attachment to others / ability to have healthy relationships

Again, change is absolutely possible; there are wonderfully inspirational stories of people who, in their thirties through their eighties, are reframing their personal narratives and growing in profound ways. But these people will likely tell you that the change was not without tremendous exertion. It's hard to overcome a difficult childhood. A healthy childhood, on the contrary, is a balm and a gift. Read over the list again. Character, good habits, faith, relational health—childhood is the box these gifts come in. These are the things we wish for the children we love.

It's not just a cute or trendy idea to save childhood. When we gift our kids childhood (the space and nurture to grow in a healthy way), *we are in fact changing history*. We are helping to develop human beings who are brave and self-sacrificing and have integrity, who appreciate and care for the earth, who defend the rights of the weak, who have been loved and are able to love, who've developed the intellectual focus to forge new territories in medicine and engineering and politics, who have soaked up the good old books and written some new ones, and who can lead countries and companies and families.

When we save childhood, we are literally shaping the next generation.

3

For years I have loved the words *let them be kids*, so it was a no-brainer to use those words as the title of this book. But as the ideas started forming themselves into stories and chapters, I realized I needed to offer some perspective for the title and a little bit of explanation. The best way I can do that is to tell you about our garden.

We are epic failures at gardening. Aside from that one summer it rained every day at 4:30 p.m. for twenty-two minutes like a heavenly sprinkler system, producing vines and vines of beautiful, delicious tomatoes, we barely *ever* produce a respectable crop. Every year I think, *This is the last year! We are never doing a garden again.* I know what I'm saying is not very on-trend, but I am telling you, we are horrible gardeners. We start out strong: we take the family trip to Lowe's, we pick out our favorite plants, we till up the soil and plant those puppies in the raised bed in the backyard. And we water it . . . *for about a week.*

Then life takes over, and it becomes too much to keep a garden alive. Once in a while I'll suddenly remember it. My son will be midbite in his bowl of oatmeal, and I'll yell, "Go water the garden!" and he'll scurry out the door. And then nothing for long stretches of time. Every third Sunday my husband will weed and pick out a few peppers, but generally we do nothing. We plant it and just let it be a garden. We let it be.

As it turns out, you can't just plant a garden and let it be. Turns out if that's all you do, the bugs eat your cucumbers, and your tomato vines get all shrively and crusty looking. Then when you look out the window at the garden, you feel this angsty sort of guilt because instead of growing a beautiful and bountiful harvest, you've slacked your way into an embarrassing and guilt-producing hobby.

That's what happens when you just plant a garden and let it be a garden. Do you know where I'm going with this?

Back to *let them be kids*, that phrase I love so much. It makes me think about climbing trees, reading good books, and the tender waiting by the washing machine for a beloved stuffed friend to come out clean and warm. It's remembrances of draping sheets and cushions every which way to make an epic living room fort and getting chased around the house by a daddy tickle-monster. It gets me choked up to think about what a gift my own childhood was. And it excites me now to think about allowing my kids to be carefree and wild. Kids should be kids!

But I'll shoot it to you straight. To let them be kids isn't simply disengaging; it costs something, often something resembling a whole stinking lot of work. You might get sweaty and dirty, your muscles might ache, but, most importantly, you can't forget about it for a single day because it needs food and water to grow. It is a whole thing.

So when I proclaim, "Let them be kids!" it is mostly *not* passive. It is *not* an exhausted resigning of duties, a last-gasp, fizzling at the end of day, free-range, unsupervised, "Oh, what the heck . . ." free-for-all. To let them be kids, we must be adults. When we let them be kids, we are the gardeners working faithfully so childhood can grow. And our work is worth it.

As I type this at the kitchen table, the three most precious things in the whole world to me are upstairs. One is rocking in the old gray chair, feet dangling, reading a novel. One is fully dressed up in doctor gear, preparing her tools for this afternoon's appointments. And one is building a climbing wall out of LEGOs. "Do you want to come up and see it, Mom?" he asks with sweet excitement.

This is a book about making space for LEGO creations, stuffed-animal doctor visits, and afternoons of careless reading. It's about saving time for family and making homemade bike ramps in the front yard. It's about the awkward school photos, cul-de-sac games of baseball, and mud soup on the sidewalk. It's about preserving make-believe and mistakes, board games and dressing like Spider-Man to go to the grocery store. This is a book about preserving childhood. Let them be kids.

I'm so glad you've joined me on this journey as we remember what we loved most about childhood and dream about how to give the very best gifts to our own kids. You'll notice that this book has a unique setup. I cover ten "gifts of childhood." Instead of one long, rambling chapter for each gift, I've divided them into a few shorter essays.

If Life Is a Garden, Then Study Your Plants

I have yet to manage a successful garden. Honestly, it seems totally overwhelming to keep thirty-six little plants alive when it takes so much energy to keep my own three children alive. But I am slowly growing in my understanding of botany through indoor potted plants purchased at Trader Joe's.

Here's how it went down. I walked in, and beautiful little green things in very Joanna Gaines–looking pots beckoned me, saying, "Take us home! You won't kill us. We're easy." Given my track record with gardening, the odds were stacked against these poor guys. And not surprisingly, I have killed half a dozen or so.

Then there was the Plant That Changed Everything. My mother-in-law gave me a clipping of her Swedish ivy vine, claiming it was "trouble free." I quickly became attached to the little meandering vine with round leaves. Originally, this plant's great-grandmother lived in the White House with President John F. Kennedy! Can you believe it? My mother-in-law had been passed down clippings from a friend, and then I got more clippings. John F. Kennedy's plant's granddaughter was doing okay for a good long while, and then . . . the telltale signs. Brown leaves. Yellowish hue. Leaves drooping. I was killing another one!

This loss wasn't going to be okay. I was tired of walking past my sad, unhealthy plants feeling like a Bad Plant Mother. The mishandling of houseplants under my watch was going to end. I did what any modern, self-respecting woman would do. I got on my laptop and googled "How do you keep houseplants alive?" and "Why are my plants dying?"

What I realized is that I had been going through the motions with my houseplants, doing things that I thought plants needed. But as it turns out, plants are persnickety. You actually have to pay attention to them individually, looking at the leaves and soil, noticing what each one needs, and watching how each responds to its environment. During this research, I learned what the rest of you probably already know: overwatering is the leading cause of death of houseplants. I learned to identify the signs of overwatering but also the signs of insufficient watering and how to tell if the plant doesn't have enough drainage.

And then I started watching my plants. Really paying attention and adjusting my care accordingly.

I realized that I had been mindlessly dumping water. In fact, the plant on the piano was sitting in an inch of water! The two in the bedroom were not getting nearly enough sun. One plant's roots were exposed, another needed a different pot, and so on and so on. The fascinating thing was that even some of the same species—the ones whose care you *thought* you could predict—needed different kinds of care.

In just a few days I began to see the fruits of my labors. It was incredibly satisfying. Instead of seeing sorry, limp plants that were losing leaves by the week, I saw happy little plants with bright green foliage.

The parallel was not lost on me.

If a simple houseplant flourishes with individualized care and attention, how much more do our children?

⋆

This book includes many of the essential ingredients to grow healthy kids: the water, light, and fertilizers of childhood. But children, like plants, are particular. They need watching. You can't assume that what worked for the first one will work for the next. And most importantly, you can't just bring them home, plop them down, and go on with your business.

I had to toss one of my houseplant casualties in the trash yesterday. It didn't make it. But that's okay; no big deal. We will all move on. Children, on the other hand, matter immensely. These infinitely complex human beings have been gifted to us to steward and nurture. The stakes are extremely high. Our calling to care for them is one of the greatest we will ever receive in this life.

As you read through the stories and tips, remember two things:

1. **It is an incredible honor to care for your children, a deep and (I believe) God-given calling with eternal ramifications.** I can guess that you are tuned in to the seriousness of this calling since you bothered to pick up a book like this. You're doing step one already, so pat yourself on the back. You are giving child-raising the appropriate honor and virtue it deserves and doing so in the face of a culture that can make you feel as if there are a million other things more or as equally important. But you get it. Way to go, you!

2. **You must watch your children and be willing to totally change things up.** Here's an analogy. I homeschool our kids. Do you know how many homeschooling philosophies there are? Hundreds! You can be a classical, traditional, Charlotte Mason, "unschooling," or Montessori homeschooler, just to name a very few. Between you and me, I don't even know what some of those words mean. For a good half a year I legit thought that Charlotte Mason had something to do with Mason jars. Turns out she's a person (RIP, Charlotte Mason). I have always thought it was a little silly to irrevocably commit to one of these philosophies. How do you know all of your kids will thrive with this or that particular formula? How do you know your children's needs will not change? How do you know (*gasp!*) that one day you may not scrap the whole thing and send them to school?

I have tried to hold my theories and practices loosely. And to regularly evaluate each child and see what he or she needs for the next season. I ask you to do the same. The goal isn't a philosophy. It's being able to walk by all your plants and your children and see them flourishing because you've paid attention to their individual needs.

I believe what I say in this book is truth, but it is not formula. The good news is, so much of parenting can be learned. I was bad at plants, and now I am not-so-bad. We can pay attention and learn and grow and become good caretakers of the plants and the children who live in our houses. It just takes some effort and not being afraid to get our hands dirty.

How to Not Hate Me When You're Reading This Book and How It Can Best Help You

I know without a shadow of a doubt that the words in this book are true. I believe in this message. But I also know that it doesn't matter as much whether these words are true as whether they become true for you. Whether they *feel like* they can be true for you.

A mom I follow on social media will post every so often about her wonderful (-ly annoying) tradition in which her kids work together to tidy the house at the end of the day. It's hard to put into words what these posts do to me.

At first, I feel disbelief. What kind of a ten-year-old boy smiles like that while he vacuums? Then I feel embarrassed, remembering the last time I asked someone to vacuum; I might just as easily have asked them to scoop up five pounds of sugar, granule by granule. Then, if I'm being totally honest, I start feeling a little mad at this mom. Does she think she's better than us because her kids enjoy scrubbing toilets? She does! She's proud! The nerve! At the tail end of all these feelings comes plain old discouragement. I am a failure at making my kids clean. Sigh. And I return to my uncleaned house with even more self-doubt and loneliness.

All of this negativity is terribly misplaced, and, of course, it's wrong of me. This mom is doing a wonderful thing. She is proud of herself, and she should be proud of herself. Her cleaning tradition took a lot of work and time and patience, and her kids have learned an extremely laudable skill. One that it would behoove mine to learn as well.

But it hurts to be reminded of something you're not doing very well. Some of us are not good at certain parts of parenting. Some of us have gotten into habits, ones that we kind of know are negative ones, but we think our kids will not respond well to change.

This is crucial. If you read this book cover to cover and all you let it do is reaffirm you in the things you are already doing, then, quite honestly, you should have used the time and money you spent on something else, like decluttering your attic and buying an over-priced drink at Starbucks. See, the real value comes when we grow in areas in which we are weak. And the real treasure is that we *can* grow in areas in which we are weak.

Last week I saw my Insta-hero ~~bragging~~ sharing about her end-of-day cleaning successes, and for once I changed the story and let her words inspire me to action. I started by speaking to myself instead of listening to myself. Instead of bemoaning and judging, I made myself say, "I could do that too."

When I woke up the next morning, I had a chance to put this new thing into practice. As it turned out, I needed help. I had 729 things to do and no good reason why my three able-bodied children couldn't help me knock some of those things off the list. I sat them down and shared my heart—which is a modern way of saying I was honest with them that I was dog-tired and overwhelmed at all the things we needed to do before our beach vacation. I told them we were a family, and families help one another. I wrote out a list of specific chores they each had to do. And then I followed through and held them accountable. Oh, but this is the worst part. We were all novices at this, so I had to overlook some growling, break up some arguments, teach someone how to make a bed correctly, hug and encourage and scold and remind. It was hard work, but at the end of it I had a clean house (not altogether notable) but also something else (extremely notable): *I had children who had grown in a skill that they desperately needed to grow in.* The satisfaction from this was immense.

I am about to share a lot of ideas in these pages. Some will be completely foreign to you and yours, and it will feel as laughable and obnoxious as the kid with the vacuum on social media. You may find themes that make your skin prickle and your eyes roll—things that make you want to shut the book and make fun of me. *Don't.* Not because I am afraid of that but because that anger sensation signals an opportunity for growth.

My anger at the Instagram mom was actually my own deep-down gut telling me that my kids *could* fold their own laundry and that they should not run outside to be swinging or fighting on the swing set while I'm overwhelmed with household chores. In the same way, any negative feelings you experience may be your gut telling you that a change needs to happen in your home. Sometimes when we feel a vague or not-so-vague sense of anger at someone else, it is because we want to make a change.

As you read, if something pricks at you and you want to disregard it, first ask yourself this question: *Do I want to make a change in this area?* Strip the emotions out of it. Answer honestly: Do you want a change? If so, here is what I advise:

- **Do something immediately.** I learned this from Cindy Rollins, who says if mothers worry that they're not doing something they should be doing, "Get up right now and do that thing. . . . Once we took a nature walk in a raging storm to quell the frustration in my heart at our lack of nature walks."[6] My tendency is to throw a weeklong pity party / analysis paralysis and then make a giant twenty-seven-step plan to fix what needs fixed. Perhaps we are better suited to just immediately put the thing into action in a small, real-life way. Kids haven't played outside in a while? Turn off the TV and make everyone go on a bike ride.
- **Be honest and forthcoming with your kids even if it means explaining that you were wrong.** Explain your new way of thinking. Apologize for the past. Tell them it will be hard for you too.

- **Be the parent.** I confess to you that sometimes I have this inexplicable difficulty making my kids do undesirable things like fold a load of towels. It's just way easier to let them keep jumping on the trampoline or whatever. I probably need counseling to figure out where that's all coming from, but I so often have to remind myself, "Don't be afraid. *You are the mom.* You know they need to do this. Be the parent."

- **Don't be afraid of resistance.** Building character in kids is work. It is painful sometimes, like listening to kids read aloud for those first few months or disentangling an argument and procuring an apology. It's returning stolen items to a friend and apologizing to the mom, helping someone re-mop a floor that was clearly dry under the chairs, sitting at home with a punished child when it would have been far easier to do the fun thing. You're not alone, and you may yet feel that deep-down confidence (sometimes very, very deep down) that you have done the right thing.

- **Remember that no one is starting from a blank slate.** I mean, maybe one or two of you in the cosmos are. And if you're one of them, we need to pause right now and give you the accolades you deserve. Yes, if you are reading this on some cozy (quiet) sofa, pregnant or not-yet-pregnant with your first child, soak in this moment. You can't see us, but we are all standing up, across states and years, saluting you right now for being an A+ proactive visionary of a (future) parent. Because you, my one-in-a-million friend, are doing what most of us did not do. The majority of moms reading (as well as the one writing) have *already begun* our habits over years, even decades of actual parenting choices. And what that means is that we have done some things right, and we have done some things wrong—or rather *are doing* some things well and some things not so well.

It is a myth, dear reader, to believe that we read these types of books from the architectural blueprint stage of parenthood. More often we have already built a large part of the house, and we are living in it. People are already eating dinner in the breakfast nook and sleeping in the (unfinished) bedrooms; there are lights flickering and appliances humming. And we look at the plywood and say, I should have built that wall a little differently. I should have chosen a different material there, or that part of the house is really not doing what it needs to be doing. The beauty of it is, *we can make changes.* We aren't living in immovable, eternally permanent, cement-wall, cinder block homes. We can do the work to straighten the crooked walls, level out the windowsills, rip up the crappy carpet, and install the new hardwoods we know we need. We can make changes in our homes.

It's Not Too Late for You

One of my living heroes is Tricia Goyer. First of all, to date, she's written seventy-two books. To date I have written exactly one and a half books, and I have whined loudly the whole time, scraping up the deep-down rudiments of my inner core to finish each painful chapter. Tricia is clearly a superstar in this element.

She is also a rock star mom. Although I know she'd grimace at that title, here is why I know it's true. She and her husband were past the baby-raising, carpooling, dirty-dishes stage of life. Her kids had all been successfully ushered into adulthood, and as parents they'd reached the stage where they were ready to relax and surely deserved to. But *instead*! Instead of reveling in newfound freedom, Tricia and her husband began again. They fostered then adopted several sibling groups. By the time it was all said and done, they added a second batch of seven older kids to the Goyer name, many of whom came carrying a tremendous amount of hurt and pain. These were children who likely had not received a childhood like the one I am idealizing in this book.

What I find encouraging and fascinating is both that these kids were able to grow, mature, and heal and how this healing came about. Tricia chose to homeschool the kids because her time with them was so short and because she wanted them to experience the blessings of home as much as they could. What did this time look like? The kids spent their school days being read to, cooking in the kitchen, playing outside, riding their bikes, and traveling together. She speaks of how the kids balked at first but eventually came to cherish this time. I don't want to simplify the story or the ending. I am sure that healing and transition after adoption can be a terribly difficult and long road. But the point I want to highlight here is that, in a way, these kids were able to "back up" and enjoy the innocent elements of childhood. I suspect they *needed* to, in order to heal.[7]

Most of us are not raising children who carry a past with profound levels of trauma. (Although some of us are, and to those of you, I say a prayer that you feel the strength for this incredible job. You have my deep respect.) But while many of us are not raising children who experienced complex trauma, none of us have unvarnished children with perfect habits.

We have children for whom we wish we could do this differently or that differently. We have kids who have seen things we wish they hadn't seen or know things we wish they didn't know. We have kids who have developed habits we wish they hadn't developed. We may be tempted to feel we are reading some of this too late to help.

Thankfully, this is not true.

Even if you are reading this as a thirtysomething grown-up, it is not too late for *you* to change. It is not too late for you to have adventures, to break unhealthy technology habits, to resurrect play and imagination, to return balance and manners and faith to your life. *And if it is not too late for you, it is certainly not too late for them.*

This is because three things are true.

1. We can learn, or relearn, how to enjoy simple pleasures.
2. We can build new habits.
3. Innocence can be restored.

For instance, kids who have been addicted to video games can become unaddicted and instead learn to love being outside. Kids who never enjoyed children's classics such as *Little House on the Prairie* or *The Boxcar Children* can learn to read them and enjoy them. Even kids who don't have grit or manners can learn either—or both.

There is hope for childhood. Not in the abstract, blank slate of future children but in *your* children, the ones in your home.

As you read, promise me that you will not lose hope. The virtues you read about here are powerful and real and worth fighting to regain. Do not despair. Change is possible.

CHAPTER TWO

THE GIFT OF ADVENTURE

Bringing Back Skinned Knees,

Secret Forts, and Yard Games

When I was in college, I volunteered my time to be a Young Life leader for high school kids. You need to know that this was totally out of character for me. Why? Because Young Life leaders tend to be crazy, fun, confident, adventurous, joy-filled sorts of people. None of those words would have described College Freshman Jessica. Mostly, I was this timid, reserved, sheltered, private-school perfectionist type. Suddenly I was thrust into a whole new world of laughter, crazy skits, loud and unruly public-school ninth graders, and the most fun I had ever had in my entire life. Being a Young Life leader was the best decision I've ever made. It gave me my husband, a big dose of confidence, great memories, and just about all of my closest friends. And it reminded me what the Good Life is.

The organization of Young Life anchors their mission in a Bible verse found in John 10:10, where Jesus said, "I have come that they may have life, and have it to the full." Here's what that anchor verse meant for us who were Young Life leaders back in western Pennsylvania in 2006: We wanted to show kids the Good Life. The really Good Life. We wanted to show them that the ways they were trying to find life and fun and happiness were not fulfilling them, but that they *could* find fulfillment in discovering that they were made by a Creator for a purpose.

The high school where we served was filled with troubled kids who had been drinking themselves into stupors, performing sexual acts in closets, and overdosing on OTC meds to numb the pain of abusive dads. Some had lost moms to cancer and others had caught their parents in affairs. We invited them to join us and through some whacky events showed them real, honest-to-goodness fun. We did crazy things like sing "Sweet Home Alabama" at the top of our lungs. We stuffed marshmallows into our mouths and sang the alphabet. They watched us dress up like redneck lumberjacks, sumo wrestlers, pocket-protector-wearing nerds, and country hobos. We danced around the stage like absolute crazy people, and they laughed until tears ran down their faces. We made them wrap toilet paper around themselves and hang Christmas ornaments on their ears. We made them square dance to mountain bluegrass music. We made them climb mountains and whitewater raft and get up at 5:00 a.m. to watch the sunrise.

As Young Life leaders we didn't invent the good stuff. No, we just spent hours praying that Jesus would fill us with his joy, then we held these kids' hands, brought them to the cliff, and showed them—with bated breath—what the Good Life could be.

When I say that kids today need adventure, it's not a side point or a peripheral idea. It's not that I needed a chapter and thought up some superfluous content to fluff up the book. No, I've included adventure, and actually put it first, because it is essential. Adventure, built into the Good Life, is actually the basis for this book. It also encapsulates our family's mission.

Your kids need to see the Good Life. They need to have lived it, breathed it, and tasted it. They need to climb the mountains, see the views, experience the sweaty foreheads and skinned-up knees from a bona fide, heart-racing adventure. The world throws so much crap at them. Imitation fun. Phony entertainment. Fake joy. The world not only throws it at them but kids are eating it up hook, line, and sinker. Depression and anxiety are at sky-high, unprecedented levels. While kids have access to higher levels of entertainment than any prior generation, they are far more bored and dissatisfied. They are the most technologically connected generation ever, but they report more loneliness.

For one example, a sobering 2019 *New York Times* article revealed that children today are more depressed than they were during the Great Depression and more anxious than they were at the height of the Cold War. Think about that for a moment; it's a staggering statistic. The article cites a study published in the *Journal of Abnormal Psychology*:

> Between 2009 and 2017, rates of depression rose by more than sixty percent among those ages fourteen to seventeen, and forty-seven percent among those ages twelve to thirteen. This isn't just a matter of increased diagnoses. The number of children and teenagers who were seen in emergency rooms with suicidal thoughts or having attempted suicide doubled between 2007 and 2015.

The article concludes, "To put it simply, our kids are not O.K."[1]

Childhood is oh-so-short. These precious years should be the time to fill them to the brim with all the excitement and joy life has to offer, instead of compounding the problem with early introductions to mental illness and unhappiness.

I do get that these eighteen years can drag on terribly (sleepless baby nights and middle school hormones—I'm looking at you). I want you to understand that I am not rocketing out of bed like, "What kind of adventure can we go on today, kids?" It's not the face of our home; it's more like the skeleton, underneath and deep down, giving shape to things.

We mate the socks and watch *Wheel of Fortune* and eat turkey sandwiches and do other boring life things other people do. But underneath it all, my husband and I yearn to show our children the Good Life. In the following pages I'm going to unpack a few qualities of the adventurous Good Life. Though there may be more, I've identified five.

1. risk and independence
2. laughter
3. nature
4. challenge and success
5. newness

Each one of these will help offer your child a chance to experience the gift of adventure, but not just your kids; I think you're going to enjoy them as well.

Risk and Independence

Kids need to experience thrill, and they will, one way or another. You can either provide the space and example for healthy outlets, or they will find it in other ways. While all kids need it, some require more than others. If you're familiar with the Enneagram personality types, you'll know that as an Enneagram six, my core emotion is fear, which causes me to spend large amounts of time and energy fleeing real or perceived dangers. I'm not what you would technically call a thrill seeker. I say this so you will take my personal examples of risk taking with a large granule of salt and not laugh too terribly hard at my expense.

When I was in college, some of my friends had a tradition that involved plastic reindeer decorations, the kind people place in their yards to spruce them up for Christmas. We would drive into town at night, and when we spotted a yard with reindeer, the guys would jump out of the car, run into the yard, and position the reindeer into amusing arrangements. Then they would sprint back to the car to get the heck out of Dodge. I'll leave it to your imagination to visualize what kinds of positions college guys would invent for plastic reindeer. (Mom and Dad, listen to me. I promise I was never directly responsible for the reindeer maneuvering. I was only the driver!) The thrill that this sheltered eighteen-year-old college girl got out of being the getaway driver for such unseemly activities was immense.

I'm not holding this activity up as the pinnacle of community service exactly, but as far as Potential Misbehaviors for College Kids, I would say it classifies as fairly benign.

College was full of these kinds of adventures. One Friday night my friend Katie and I snuck into our guy friends' dorm rooms and did outrageous things like make their beds (oh, the craziness!). We left them cryptic notes, stole their ramen noodles, and interviewed their roommates. I will say that my husband's list of "adventures I had in college" is way more interesting, but my kids may read this book one day, and I don't want to give them any of those ideas. My point is, being sneaky is just about one of the most fun feelings one can have. Isn't that interesting? We were made for adventure.

I absolutely love how my Hawaiian friend Monica Swanson, the author of *Boy Mom*, describes it. She believes in fiercely protecting her boys' hearts but giving them immense freedom to take physical risks.

> While I am deeply concerned about protecting my boys' hearts, my husband and I believe strongly in encouraging them to experience healthy adventures and appropriate risks. When he was eleven years old, our son Luke started surfing giant waves at beaches known for potentially deadly conditions. (He had trained for it, I promise.) All our boys are avid spear fishermen who spend summer days diving deep in the ocean with powerful spearguns. . . . We give them freedoms to face reasonable risks.[2]

As a worrier (see previous page), I kind of gulp at the idea of my sons spearfishing in deep waters. It's ironic, though, because I have a gut feeling those deepwater adventures Monica's boys prep for are far less dangerous than letting kids hang out "safely" indoors with a bunch of technology.

How can we help our kids find thrill the right way? The possibilities are nearly endless and can vary depending on where you live and what kinds of resources you have around, but here are a few good old standbys:

- flashlight tag, capture the flag, laser tag, or paintball games
- scavenger hunts (My uncle once created elaborate, personalized hunts for each of us to find our Easter baskets on my

grandparents' one-hundred-acre horse farm. We had the best time. I still remember some of the clues!)

- challenging physical activities, such as skiing, sledding, mountain biking, rafting, ropes courses, and skating
- any number of outrageous contraptions or concoctions your kids create that seem a little bit dangerous

Ah, yes. That last one: kids are actually experts at inventing their own ways to test their limits. Building bike ramps out of mounds of dirt, creating a roller coaster with pillows down the stairs, skateboarding down their mattresses, rappelling down the banister with belts tied together. I don't want to be labeled as sexist or anything, but in my personal experience boys in particular are oddly brilliant at devising these types of situations. My instinctive reaction to these things is usually some version of "Gah! That's not safe. Please stop right now!" But the truth is, we must allow them to take risks in a healthy way and fulfill their inborn longings for adventure so we're there to process it with them and help them learn.

One time after it snowed, the adventurous kids in the neighborhood constructed a giant snowboarding jump in someone's front yard. Which was fine, except that the conveniently located peak for the jump was actually a power transformer with large signs plastered all over that said, "Caution! Do not touch!" So we had a little talk about (1) reading posted warnings and (2) respecting electrical power—which are good reminders. Before you let them go be wild ones in the great big world, it's a fabulous idea to provide hard-and-fast boundaries for things that are always off-limits. A "family code of ethics for play," if you will. Here are some ideas:

- It is off-limits to inflict pain on people or animals.
- It is off-limits to damage or destroy property that does not belong to you.

- It is off-limits to make someone do something that he or she does not want to do.
- It's off-limits to do something that an adult has already told you not to do.
- You have a good brain inside your head. Use it. If something seems like a bad idea, maybe it is.
- If you need help, I'm here for you.

Once your kids know the rules, you give them some space and let them play.

You know what's really awesome? Finding adventures that either

1. show kindness to someone else, or
2. require bravery to help someone.

You may have to help them think up some of these. Think along the lines of a *drive-by* blessing, where you leave a gift or gift card on the doorstep of someone who needs it, ring the doorbell, and sprint out of sight. It's like toilet-papering someone's house, but opposite. One twist on this is Saint Nicholas Day Candy Caning. Since Saint Nicholas was known for his generosity, on December 6 (Saint Nicholas Day) you find a family who could use some love. You drive to their house after dark, sneakily poking real candy canes into the ground or into flowerpots on their front porch. You leave a gift on the doorstep, ring the doorbell, and jet out of sight. My friend who shared this tradition commented that her boys felt so sneaky doing this activity, like stealthy Navy SEALs. It gave them such a rush. What a gift to give kids—the thrill of adventure *and* the thrill of helping someone. My kids still talk about the time we found a baby bird floundering in the pool and fished it out with pool noodles and skimming nets. We had to scoop it up into a plastic dive-toy box, and then we walked it home in the baby stroller to nurse it back to health. For three- and five-year-old boys, this amounted to an absolutely epic adventure to help save the little bird. (Between you and me, the bird disappeared from the garage while we were eating dinner, and I doubt he had learned to fly that quickly. I just had to get that off my chest.)

As your kids get older, independence is a sister to adventure. I think kids get antsy and moody when they're aching for more independence. My oldest was about eight years old when I noticed he was just not himself, bored and out of sorts. "Buddy, how would you like to ride your bike around the neighborhood . . . alone?" His eyes lit up like fireflies. He'd never been able to do that. I sent him out with a reminder of a few rules and worst-case-scenario solutions (I can't help myself), and off he went. His mood improved dramatically. Age-appropriate independence, with a hefty dose of "Wow, what a big kid you are now!" fulfills all sorts of needs inside of children. This is different from no supervision or just ignoring them to do whatever the heck they want. Rightful independence says, "I see you. I notice who you are, and what you're capable of. This is a new challenge, and you're up to it. I'll be right over here if you need me."

Not long ago the boys and their cousins discovered that if they climbed the fence behind my sister's yard, there was a whole long strip of uninhabited land full of overgrown bushes, streams and puddles, discarded treasures, snakes (this was never confirmed but imagined), rabid foxes (same), and bears (I mean . . . it could happen, right?). The boys christened this strip of land Manland, much to the severe disappointment of their outnumbered girl-cousin Katie, who begged for a more politically correct name, like Peopleland (but was overruled).

The kids loved Manland so much. They begged to go to Manland every day. They cried literal tears when they couldn't go.

What was so great about it? One boy ended up with a case of poison ivy so bad he needed oral steroids. Several kids ripped their pants and were caked with mud and wet to the bone. It was literally just an overgrown piece of deserted property.

But they were alone. They were adventuring, unsupervised. Growing kids need their own versions of Manland. A place to pretend and risk and create. A Roxaboxen sort of place to build their own villages and colonies. And when one Manland feels dull and childish and ends up deserted, then they need room to forge a new road and find a new one. These are the adventures that make a childhood.

Laughter

I mentioned earlier I was a Young Life leader during college. One summer I invited some of the high school girls I knew to go to Young Life camp with me in the Adirondack Mountains of New York. These particular girls were knee-deep in some tough stuff. How do I put this? There wasn't a lot of playing Scrabble or baking cookies going on at this juncture of their lives.

They agreed to go to camp with me. The second night we were there, I told them to put on their flannel shirts because we were going to a square dance. They looked at me as if I were a space alien. It took a lot of maneuvering and debating, but I finally got them out the door.

We arrived at the old barn, where two guys dressed like rednecks were strumming banjos and slapping their knees. I was getting a few really evil side-eyes when the banjo guys started yelling instructions. "Two by two! Swing your partner, round and round!" In ten minutes the whole room of high schoolers had been transformed into an old-fashioned, barn-raising square dance party. And these. Kids. Loved. It. There was not a person in the room who wasn't smiling. This was real fun, through and through. More fun than the fun they had been having, for sure.

So few kids enjoy real laughter today. Sure, they know how to make fun of someone. They know how to scoff or mock. They know how to be sarcastic. Oh boy, do they know that! But to simply laugh—to be overcome with pure, unadulterated joy—it is one of the best gifts of life and is enjoyed so infrequently. It's good to begin introducing this kind of fun to our children now, so they don't have to wait until their teenage years to realize real joy is better than the illicit things they might get involved in.

I remember when it dawned on me that I had the power to introduce my children to joy. I struggled a lot as a new mom with the isolation and postpartum depression and anxieties. Then one day I had a revelation. I was feeding my son pureed peaches with rice and chicken. (Don't judge; it's a thing!) I was playing peek-aboo, and he was laughing hysterically, the kind of baby belly laugh that would make even the Grinch smile. He was having the best time. And it dawned on me: he won't laugh unless I make him laugh. He could go the whole day without laughing, but if I make him laugh, then he'll enjoy laughter that day. It seems like a really silly thing to dawn on someone, I guess. But the profound responsibility, if I can call it that, that I owned to bring him joy—*it was empowering*. I had the power to make that sweet little baby laugh until his belly hurt, or to sit bored and unoccupied all day in a baby chair.

This little boy went on to grow up (the nerve), and now he laughs without me. He has jokes shared with his friends or that he's read in a book. But even now, as the mother—the keeper of the home, the playdate maker, the activity chooser, the controller of the remote, the setter of the passwords, and the owner of the devices—I am the biggest influencer in my children's lives. I can use this influence in a powerful way.

Following are a few ways you can encourage real joy and laughter in your home:

- **Have a zero-tolerance policy for sarcasm.** I guess as they grow up, you can lax this policy, but have you noticed that small children do not understand sarcasm? It is hurtful and confusing to them. I tend to enjoy sarcasm, personally, and I remember the first time I tried it with one of my kids. It was a giant flop. I remember the hurt in his eyes. What this also means is that you don't invite company over via TV and YouTube who are mean and sarcastic for humor. Adults understand this but kids do not. Same thing goes for laughing at someone's expense. Your home should be a safe place from mean humor.

- **Tell funny stories.** I find the weighty distractions of real life to be quite distracting from humor. This is why God gave me my husband. For my part, I am constantly occupied by finding someone's water bottle, or locating someone a clean pair of socks, or remembering to turn the rice down so the fire department doesn't come again (true story). I get really distracted by these things and I don't stop and joke with my kids. But every time I do, I see their faces light up and wonder why I don't get silly more often.

- **Enjoy real, quality entertainment that is funny.** See my suggestions for books and movies in Resources. For now, here are a few books that make us laugh: *Garfield* comic books, *Ginger Pye*, *Winnie-the-Pooh*, and the Hank the Cowdog series.

- **Don't underestimate the tickle factor.** Fussy babies, grumpy toddlers, moody fourth graders, and unsuspecting husbands . . . it's amazing how a sneaky tickle attack just changes the entire vibe in the home. Try it!

Laughter brings out the best in us. It brightens the day, lightens our load, and lifts our spirits. Don't let a day go by without sharing the gift of laughter with your kids. You'll never be sorry you did.

Nature

A few years ago my husband and I got an inkling that RV camping would be a perfect fit for our family. Our longings do not always match. His dream birthday party, for example, is batting away mosquitos while fly fishing in the middle of Nowhere, Tennessee; mine is an epic gathering of my seventy-five closest friends in a high-end uptown restaurant. But in the case of the proposed RV hobby, we aligned. For me, it seemed the perfect way to have adventures while remaining in the safe and cozy confines of our own sanitized and well-organized property (I'm not a control freak at all). For him, well . . . the fly fishing thing again.

We scrimped and saved and dreamed and planned, and after three years, the perfect camper for our family was for sale fifty miles away. It was used, but the toilet wasn't disgusting (which is very important), and it had been on the market for almost a year, so it was priced at rock bottom. We did it! We were ecstatic. This was the year that it rained every weekend for seven straight months, so we had to maintain our enthusiasm over half a year, but we kept it steady.

The first time we parked the RV in front of our house in anticipation of a weekend trip, I texted the whole neighborhood to come tour it, and a few kind friends gushed with me: the kitchen table turns into a bed! An outdoor sink. Three bunk beds. I cleaned that thing from top to bottom, which is how I show things I love them.

The next twenty-four hours involved the buying or relocating of one of nearly everything we use on a daily basis from our house to our camper. I don't wear a Fitbit, but if I did, I think it would have exploded. Then you have to arrange it all in the camper so that it can survive a jaunt at 70 mph, which includes a lot more sweating and bungee cords and jamming things into closets. Then you have to pack all the food you'll need for three days and all the utensils you'll need to cook them. Then you have to hook the camper to the truck. At this point I was appointed out of necessity to be the lookout while my husband backed up the truck. My marriage barely survived this step. Evidently there is a whole language for telling someone how to move a vehicle, and I am not proficient in this language. I would be motioning him to back up (clear as day, y'all), and he would go forward! Or I'd point to go left, and he'd go right.

All that to say, by the time the family was buckled in the truck and all the necessary valves and latches were attached that were supposed to be attached, Todd and I said things to each other like, "We just packed up our entire house and are lugging it behind us to a campsite. Why do people do this? Have we been duped?" I think there was more of a back-and-forth snipping and arguing to it if I'm being honest. (Did I mention how hot and sweaty we were?)

Then we arrived at the campground. There was a brief incident involving something called a water and sewage hookup, which I didn't realize was a thing you had to specify when reserving a campsite. Whoever heard of booking a rental house and having to tell them you wanted a toilet or running water? Alas, it's all different with camping.

But then, then the fun began. There is a reason people love camping. It is the moment after all this tomfoolery, when you're in front of a fire pit with the ones you love, God's gorgeous backyard behind you, and crickets and frogs for Pandora. It is worth it. It really and truly is! I've found this always, always to be the case with our outdoor adventures. It takes work to get there, and then the reward is tenfold.

My children come alive. I'm not just being a flowery, exaggerating author. Take it from the horse's mouth with these exact words from my son: "If we camped in a camper and ate the same hot dog dinner and a very fruity lunch and biked and played in the creek every day, it would be the best life ever."

"The best life ever." The simplicity of what they actually did stuns me. They put their bare feet in a stream, made fires, rubbed the sooty sticks on rocks, took off their shirts and splashed in a trickling waterfall. It's not the magic of Disney. The food, quite honestly, was subpar—not my best work. We didn't have a bunch of elaborate adventure equipment. We didn't do a kayaking tour or a rafting adventure or a guided hike. We just led them to a stream. More accurately, *they found* the stream, immediately, using some sort of innate navigational instinct. And then they just came alive.

Still, discerning mothers and fathers will recall the work that went into ending up near the stream (all the sweat and bungee cords and whatnot) and think, *But isn't it a lot of work to get out in nature?*

Yes and no. It is, in the sense that getting a slew of kids dressed for and schlepped to an adventure definitely requires time and energy from Mom and Dad. But it is easier in the long run because nature heals and nurtures children. I witness it in my own kids, how they come alive when they are outdoors. But it can be observed even in clinical studies. Richard Louv, author of the bestselling *Last Child in the Woods*, notes, "Studies suggest that nature may be useful as a therapy for Attention Deficit Hyperactivity Disorder (ADHD), used with or, when appropriate, even replacing medications or behavioral therapies."[3] Louv goes on to speculate that perhaps ADHD is a set of symptoms aggravated by lack of exposure to nature. He muses, "The real disorder is less in the child than it is in the imposed, artificial environment."[4]

Reflecting upon his own childhood, Louv concludes, "The woods were my Ritalin. Nature calmed me, focused me, and yet excited my senses."[5]

Okay, I'm just going to come out and say it. Your daily in-and-out life needs to allow your kids to interact with (not just view) nature. They need to be able to touch and breathe and mash and stir and pick up and splash and dig in the earth on a regular basis. Here are some practical ways you can enjoy nature in your daily life:

- **Weave traditions that bring a change of scenery into the fabric of your year.** Long ago, families who lived in cities and suburbs took whole summer-long vacations to the sea. I have always secretly wished I lived in those times. I get it; it's not like you can up and leave downtown Nashville or Houston from June to August these days and escape to the shore, but what about the smaller trips your family takes? Even those annual traditions to beautiful places are integral to a child being able to just be a child. What parent doesn't remember the satisfaction (and amazement, really) of seeing the kids dig in the sand at the beach *for hours* on end, happy as clams? (How about that for a perfect metaphor?) They dump and dig and feel the wet sand between their fingers and never seem to tire of it. This is doing more than you think for your child. Those vacations to the lake or the mountain or the beach—wherever you see your kids simply come alive outdoors—*make these happen*. Don't forget them.

- **Adopt a park nearby.** I don't mean just a place with a swing set and one of those colored, germ-infected hamster mazes for kids. (Legit, one time we found actual poop smeared *all over* a kiddie slide, and it definitely contaminated one of my kids. Wiping your kid's own poop off his legs is one thing; anonymous poop is another entirely.) So, yeah, the playground scene is not so much what I'm describing here. I'm envisioning a natural park with endless grass, full-grown trees, maybe a stream and a bridge and a trail? Find one of these. Get to know the trees; come back and notice them through the seasons. Maybe you live in an apartment or condo with no backyard. This is an excellent way to "adopt" a backyard. I know I'm not telling anyone something they don't already know, but here's my encouragement to do it more, do it as much as you can. Bring your own book and coffee and sit and watch your kids do who-knows-what. Don't feel the need to entertain or have an agenda. There is a time and a place for nature scavenger hunts, but sometimes it is good and fine to just let kids make their own adventures. For us this has led to transporting tadpoles home in plastic cups, riding home nearly naked because our clothes were wet, people getting stung by bees and stepping on ant hills, someone hot and grumpy and ready to leave before anyone else (and sometimes that "someone" is Mom). But when we give our kids time in nature, we are providing them with something so beautiful.

- **Create a *Chopped Jr.*, Nature Edition.** My kids discovered the Food Network show *Chopped Jr.* on vacation and were absolutely mesmerized. A few weeks later they reinvented this game—backyard version. It has become a whole thing in the neighborhood. They found large, flat rocks to use as plates. The "judge" specifies three ingredients they have to use for dinner. For example: rocks, leaves, and berries. Then the kids "cook" a meal using whatever the heck they can find in the yard. And let me be clear: we live in a suburban neighborhood. We don't have a prolific variety of lush greenery and beautiful wildflowers aplenty for the picking. It's your typical run-of-the-mill grass backyard. My kids have an absolute blast. And can we have a minute here for mud soup? I find it fascinating that no one has to teach kids how to make mud soup, but they nearly all do it. Whenever I happen upon a mud soup kitchen, it never fails; something is not quite right. Someone is still wearing their church clothes, or one of my favorite spatulas is being used to stir the "pancakes," or company is about to come over and the front door is getting a freshly applied coat of mud paint, dark stain version. And just so we are all clear, church clothes are at a premium around here, so you better believe those puppies are stripped off like they're on fire as soon as I see what's going on. But I always find a way to let the mud cooking proceed.

- **Invest in a bird feeder.** Fair warning: I get really sappy and grandma-like when I talk about bird feeders (with no disrespect to grandmas, with whom I have always had so very much in common). I have an absolute next-level obsession with bird feeders. They have brought such joy to our home. It's incredible the variety of birds that will gravitate to your back porch with the right kind of feed. This is an extremely low-impact way to bring nature to your kids. Pick up a local bird identification book and *boom*: homemade science lesson.

I know some of these might seem to be obvious or rather silly examples, but don't miss the forest for the trees. (I am absolutely rocking the metaphors in this chapter.) The most primary thing for you to remember is that nature heals and nurtures. Childhood is short. Take them outdoors.

Challenge and Success

The last time we visited the library, the parking lot was undergoing renovations, so instead of our usual route, we had to drive around the block and park inside an adjacent parking deck. *Really, Jessica—could you have picked a more uninteresting sentence to begin this section?* I know what you're thinking, but stick with me. This meant that my three kids and I were inside a parking deck, all twist-turned backward from our usual way of getting inside the library. Lost? Maybe a little bit.

As I had to carry the usual seventy-five pounds of Hardy Boys and nonfiction football books to return my usual two days late, I was not super pumped to take a half-mile jaunt around downtown. Then we saw it: an old metal door in the corner of the parking deck. The rusty old sign read "Library," with an arrow pointing a dubious direction. Stairwells in parking decks are on my list of top ten creepy things, but my two boys were undeterred. "Mom! Let's do it!"

The concrete stairwell smell hit us with full force. It was dark, and as the door ominously slammed behind us (maybe locked?), a solitary door loomed ahead. My boys were invigorated. "Let's try it!" We opened up to the unfamiliar backside of the library, and with quickening steps the kids raced left, then right, then straight ahead. "Yes! There it is! Mom, we found the library!" It was such a simple moment for my children, but in a weird way, it was more than that. It was an unexpected Tuesday afternoon adventure. Before you're tempted to make fun of this pathetic excuse for an adventure, hear me out. I recognize it wasn't the heart-pounding, thrill-seeking sort, but in its own right it was a mini-challenge for my kids. And we had done it. We'd navigated a new path, guessed correctly, and figured out a problem. Our steps were confident opening the doors to our next load of Hardy Boys books.

And it reminded me, those what-do-we-do-next sorts of moments are a great gift of childhood. Unless your kids find themselves in a real-life Boxcar Children situation without authority figures or anything to eat for dinner, the stakes are reassuringly low for children. In a low-pressure, low-risk, practicing sort of way, kids can try their wings, gain confidence, and solve a problem. Yes, there may be a few muddy sneakers, Band-Aids, and "You did *what*?" moments, but what is gained in children is vastly worth it. If you have a really bored and mopey kid, perhaps it's because he hasn't had a good challenge in a while.

In fact, it starts with babies and goes all the way up. I had so much to learn with my first baby. So, so much. I was not one of those women who had been an aunt forever, volunteered in the church nursery for decades, or always rushed to someone's baby to hold it and coo. I am just not (*gasp!*) a baby person. I was kind of putting all of it off until I absolutely couldn't anymore. This meant that having my own baby was an eye-opening experience, to say the least. The thing that baffled me most (and if I'm honest, frustrated me the most) was how quickly the rules all changed. I would think I had it figured out: he likes to play, nurse, and then take a twenty-minute nap. That's his routine . . . until next Wednesday, that is. It felt like the moment I had a handle on what my baby liked or needed or could do, things would change. Contrary to how it felt as a poorly adjusted postpartum mom clinging desperately to my former life of schedule and predictability, my baby was not being malicious or naughty. Quite the contrary. He was doing just what he was supposed to do; he was growing.

One day I was putting him down for his nap with his blaring-loud sound machine and swaddling him all nice and tight, and he was mad as a hornet. Screaming and fussing, he was not doing at all what he was supposed to do. My mom said (gingerly, I'm sure), "Jessica, do you think he's too old to be swaddled? What if you turn that sound down? Could you give him some toys to play with in his crib?" And I said (not gingerly, I'm sure), "*Mom*. This is what he likes. I have no idea why he's so unhappy. He never wants toys during his nap." Two guesses how this ended.

And that's how it is, the whole time being a mom. Never anticipating that my kids are actually ready for the challenges they are ready for. There are always warning signs that kids are needing a challenge, that they are bored. Not in the good boredom we will talk about in chapter 3, but in the I'm-growing-and-antsy-in-my-skin, give-me-a-challenge kind of way.

Here are a few clues that something is up:

- Your toddler rips apart the board books during naps, when what he needs is the next stage of toys.
- You put on a kiddie show such as *Wild Kratts* for your elementary-aged kids, and they end up high-jumping on the couch because the show isn't age appropriate anymore.
- Your kids are fighting nonstop for a month, and it's been raining nonstop for a month, and what everyone needs is a good change of scenery.
- You start getting a lot of eye-rolling and disgruntled groans from your soon-to-be middle schooler, and he or she needs a new thing: a challenging sport, a new hobby to immerse herself in, or perhaps his first job.

It takes a lot of watching and paying attention to be a parent. It's not something you can put on autopilot. When I was a kid, I had a fish tank shaped like Garfield, and Garfield's stomach was the glass part of the tank where you could see the fish. When we went on vacation, we bought these hard things shaped like shells that were a sort of gradually disintegrating food. You could be gone for up to two weeks with this magic! The food would release itself in chunks, and the fish lived with no supervision. Not so with parenting, literally or metaphorically. (I'm sure your kitchen sink and grocery list prove the point.)

You have to watch and adjust care. Kids are always changing and always needing the next round of nourishment, stimulation, and challenge. There are two final things to keep in mind regarding kids and a good challenge.

First, not every kid needs or wants the same challenge. Remember that part about knowing your plants? It's about watching them and sensing their boredom and readiness for the next thing. As a Christian, I find it really helpful to pray. It has been my experience that God really hears these prayers for guidance with our kids, and he'll provide answers when we ask.

And, finally, don't give up looking for challenges and success, and don't let them give up either. Being truly good at something is crucial to healthy development. Kids *need* to be successful. Help them find their thing. For some kids it is obvious. I had a son who, at age two, whacked a plastic golf club for literally hours of the day. I learned to dodge foam golf balls as I did the dishes. For other kids it takes a little more time. And it doesn't have to be their lifelong thing. Some of the cousins have a "snake-making store" that is quite serious. So many varieties of snakes are produced out of tape and construction paper and tape and scissors and tape, and did I say so much tape? It is quite a thing. This may not be their lifelong calling. (Please?) But they feel so proud of their paper snake collection, and they should be. What hard work!

My daughter and I were reading the other day about pet hamsters. The book made a big deal about how they need activities to be stimulated. They need plastic treadmills and giant rolling balls and mazes that are different colors. If a little, fluffy rodent with a yearlong life span can't survive without challenge, then certainly neither can a human being.

Newness

In the introduction I used the garden analogy for childhood. It takes some tending, I said, to grow a childhood. It's interesting to me how so much of it involves a delicate balancing of the soil. I don't understand the first thing about soil constitution, but my landscaper husband tells me if the soil doesn't stay at the correct pH, plants wither and die. Healthy plants need soil with the right balance of acid and base. The same is true for a healthy childhood; it requires a balance. Freedom and boundaries. Work and rest. Adventure and boredom. And then this one: routine and newness.

Because, yes, one of the key nutrients for childhood is the calm and reliable security of a routine.

> Meaning hides in repetition: We do this every day or every week because it matters. We are connected by this thing we do together. We matter to one another. In the tapestry of childhood, what stands out is not the splashy, blow-out trip to Disneyland but the common threads that run throughout and repeat: the family dinners, nature walks, reading together at bedtime . . . Saturday morning pancakes.[6]

But with this said, something else needs to be added. Kids, having been provided their safe and cozy routine of home, will need to experience the thrill of discovering something (or someplace) new. All of us humans enjoy a fresh perspective, but children especially relish and thrive with the discovery of *new*.

I can prove it. You know how the toys at other people's houses are always more exciting than your kids' own toys? Or how about this one: Have you ever taken your kids to a hotel? I don't mean a resort with life-sized animal statues greeting you on every floor or the walls decorated with jungle murals and stuff like that. I mean a normal, Hampton-Inn sort of situation. The first time you take kids to a plain old hotel room, what is their reaction? If your kids are like mine, from the moment you crack the door, there's pure excitement over the blandest of features. A bathroom! Two beds! A desk! And your kids will rush in like hyenas pouncing on prey, exploring the room piece by piece. Picking up the phone, jumping on the bed. Opening. All. The. Doors. And. Drawers. And then! To push the elevator button! To insert the key in the door! It's exhilarating!

It's not that Hampton Inn's furniture is better or cooler than your own. Like your neighbor's LEGO table, it's new, it's different, it's a change of scenery. I began this chapter on adventure, explaining the beauty of introducing our children to the joyous adventure that life can be. Introducing our kids to the new and different is one of those pure, unadulterated joys that lend a richness to life. A richness that is better than, say, sitting around at the mall and criticizing everyone who walks by. Or holing up in a basement for the entire day to play Candy Crush. Kids who have learned how to embrace adventure in the big, beautiful world are kids who are less lured by the lame old lusts of life.

Once you've gotten the hotel outing checked off the box (ha!), there are a million other ways to hold your kids' hands and let them experience the thrill of newness and discovery. A few everyday ways to bring the spark of discovery into your family's life might include one or more of the following ideas:

- **Experience animals.** Visit the zoo, meet new pets, go to the pet store. Animals are the most fantastic creatures. We have leopard geckos for pets, and when my neighbor met them, the first words out of her mouth were "Wow! Isn't God amazing that he makes all these creatures!"

- **Be culturally diverse.** Learn a language, or meet new friends from other cultures. Recently we invited a Chinese woman to our Saturday morning pancake breakfast. She was in the country while visiting her college-aged daughter. What an unexpected delight! I did it because I felt it was the right thing to do. But oh my goodness! It was such a treat to talk with and learn from someone from an entirely differ-ent background and culture. Before she left our house, she hugged me tight and left us with two treasures to remem-ber her by: a gorgeous genuine Chinese paper fan and a little tin of Chinese tea. Was it risky, uncomfortable, and a little awkward at times to invite a woman we'd never met, speaking a language we don't speak, over for scrambled eggs? Of course. But I'd do something like that again in a heartbeat.

- **Relish the changes outside.** When you have little children, you don't need to look far to find newness. Little kids find thrill in seeing the leaves change for fall, in the rainbow after a rain shower, the sky before a thunderstorm, how the snow melts off the roof, the different ways the moon looks throughout the month.

- **Allow them to enjoy little thrills in everyday things** that children are so good at doing. Childhood is the place that it should be safe and perfectly okay to jump up and down over a new pair of shoes. Children naturally excel at this, and we should take a lesson. There was the year I redecorated the downstairs, and we all oohed and aahed over the new wall art from Hobby Lobby. Oh, let them enjoy these little sparks of life. My kids are obsessed with the car wash. Sometimes it makes no rational sense to drive through the car wash, such as when there is a 90 percent chance of rain tomorrow, but it brings them such joy! (Just so you know, sometimes I am the lame old mom who refuses to go through the car wash because there is a 90 percent chance of rain tomorrow. But sometimes, what the heck. I do it.)

Besides the small, everyday ways to experience fresh newness in life, you can have grand family adventures. I need you to know that this does not come easily to me. I follow some moms on social media who seem to live in breathtaking, fairy-nature worlds. From what I can gather from their Instagram feeds, one of three scenarios is happening:

1. One of the parents has a job as a *National Geographic* photographer, and they basically travel around the national park scene getting next-level images of their kids fly fishing in Oregonian rivers and watching geysers go off in California.
2. They own a cattle farm in east Texas in a modern farmhouse that Joanna Gaines helped remodel, and their kids run wild on the prairies (in between helping to birth calves and harvesting the family crop).
3. They live thirty minutes from the beach and spend several days a week climbing driftwood and retrieving jellyfish from their (essentially) private beaches.

In case you couldn't read between the lines, let's make it official: I am completely jealous of scenarios one, two, and three! If you are one of these parents, please don't keep reading this chapter; just write your own book and tell us what it's like. Most of us, however, including yours truly, live very normal lives. I am a boring, suburban, stay-at-home mom, and it has taken us a lot of work to get out and give our kids grand adventures. At the risk of being overly simplistic, here is how you take an abstract goal, like "Do something cool with my kids," and make it actually happen.

Step 1: Set your goals. What is something you'd like to do with your family? Where is a place your kids have never seen that you'd like to take them? Pick three out-of-the-ordinary experiences that, at some point, you'd like your kids to have. My goodness, there are so many possibilities. Here are a few to get your wheels turning:

- Tour the Smithsonian museums.
- Whitewater raft on a river.
- Enjoy New York City at Christmas.
- See the Grand Canyon.
- Drive across the country.
- Tent camp, ride horses, mountain bike, or hike up a mountain.
- Explore a new region of the country (for example, the West Coast, the East Coast, the Great Plains, or a big city).
- Visit Yosemite National Park.

Step 2: Decide how you will get where you want to go. Decide the method of travel to your goal. RV or camper? Drive and stay in hotels? Airbnb?

Step 3: Talk it up as a family. This is the really fun part. Dream about this together. Don't miss this step, because a shared dream binds families together.

Step 4: Break it into small goals. For example, our family wants to make a long cross-country trip. Our goals started like this:

1. Save for and purchase a truck to haul a camper.
2. Save for and purchase an RV.
3. Take smaller trips to get used to RVing.
4. Plan a cross-country trip.
5. Go on a cross-country trip!

As I write this, we are on step four above. I know it may sound overly simplistic, but have you taken these steps for your family? The fun of this plan is that you can enjoy the whole process. When we think about creating grand adventures for our families, oh, that heavy load of guilt so easily can creep in. And things start to feel like a chore, another item to add to the everlasting parental to-do list. This type of guilt is not helpful. Do not look at adventure as one more thing you need to do. *Instead, look at it as a permission slip*: your permission slip to revive dull and dreary adulthood with activities that bring life and joy. Don't you miss the mountains? Don't you love the feel of the sun on your face? Don't you want to see authentic art or music up close? You don't have to take a break from these things with children. Do them *with* your children!

CHAPTER THREE

THE GIFT OF BOREDOM

Why Kids Need Mental White Space

When I was a kid, there were about four choices for yogurt. You could have the gross nonfat kind in strawberry or vanilla, or you could have the good, regular yogurt in strawberry or vanilla. The 1990s mother's brain was not tormented with rows and rows of yogurt options. Her brain did not have to waste valuable energy deciphering between options like organic, low-fat, real-sugar Greek blueberry and cultured, high protein, good-source-of-fiber, real blueberry. I know that sentence hurt your head to read, and I'm sorry; I owe you some brain cells.

Same with summer camp. When I was a kid, you had two choices for summer camp. Go, or don't go. This morning I did a seven-minute Internet search for summer camp options for a five-year-old. A five-year-old, mind you. Here is a brief, inexhaustive list of possibilities for a preschool summer camp: pottery, art, hip-hop dance, gymnastics, farm camp, basketball, drumming, 4-H fitness, LEGO, horseback riding, Spanish, cooking, and, of course, a get-ready-for-school camp.

These are the options for five-year-olds. And some, apparently, are so sought after that you have to sign up within the first few days or risk losing your spot. When you read over the list, you might feel behind, quite honestly, if your five-year-old is putzing around in a Spider Man suit while your neighbors' kids are preemptively practicing free throws.

Now, listen. I am a former educator and children's ministry director, a lover of books and projects and specially chosen classes. I certainly believe that our children's minds should be stretched and their interests followed. *However*, I also believe that boredom is one of the greatest gifts you can give to a child.

You know what I was doing during the dog days of summer when I was a kid (and by the way, much older than five)? My four cousins and I sprawled out in Aunt Marci's bedroom with a deck of cards, an FM radio, and a sleeve of saltines. From lunch until dinner we listened to Shania Twain and Diamond Rio while playing War, Spoons, and Kemps, which I still contest is one of the greatest card games a kid could ever play.

When we got sick of card games and were down to crumbs of saltines, we squirted one another in the face with a rubber bunny-shaped bath toy. I realize this example makes us sound like a bunch of unsocialized weirdos, but that's kind of the whole point. We were free. There was no one watching, no need to be "cool," nothing else we "should" or "had" to do. Nothing to Instagram or Snapchat. No millions of activities we had to be herded to and from. We could just be. It was a blissfully lame life.

There wasn't much to do, so we made stuff up. We built forts out of everything: trees, sheets, sleeping bags, boxes, dilapidated hammocks, and bales of hay (but not all at once). We would suck down a half dozen Icee Pops a day, fling the plastic at one another, and lick the sugar dye off our hands. Mom wasn't totally against TV, but there was only so much *The Price Is Right* one could stomach, so around 1:30 p.m. we'd just turn it off and find something else to do. We orchestrated a dog show, a talent show, and charged the neighborhood two dollars admission for what surely was a thoroughly amusing performance of magic tricks.

In fifth grade a group of us neighborhood girls decided to fight imaginary crime by creating a detective agency. We used old manila file folders and wrote out elaborate profiles of heinous villains. We just had nothing better to do than alphabetize the folders of imaginary Blockbuster robbers. (A little background for all you youngsters: in the past *you actually had to drive your car to a store* to rent a movie. Can you even imagine our lives?)

When there weren't any friends to play with, I decided to transform our home into a library by card-cataloguing all the books we owned. (What? Not normal?) Yes, every afternoon in sixth grade, I sprinted to the basement, rounded up a big stack of books, divided them into categories, and labeled and stamped them with the date. (P.S. My husband didn't find out about my junior-high life as a pretend librarian until after we were engaged. #sucker)

This is probably a good juncture to let you know I turned out totally normal (maybe not totally but mostly). And that's the whole point. Those seemingly childish, ridiculous, creative, imaginative games we played because we had nothing else better to do—we turned out all right, not in spite of them but *because* of them.

The cold truth is, whether we admit it or not, the generation sleeping down the hall in the bunk beds and cribs? They're a bunch of guinea pigs, plain and simple. There has not yet existed a generation who played Mickey Mouse Clubhouse on an iPhone during every single doctor's appointment of their lives. No one has yet made it to adulthood who learned to read on an iPad app or got selfie "likes" in fifth grade. A whole generation of kids is being schlepped from one traveling soccer team to afterschool tutoring to advanced violin lessons to whatever, and *who in the world knows what it's doing inside*?

We just don't know what this early stimulation does to the brain, heart, or mind. (And the little we do know is rather alarming, but I digress.)

I'll say it again: mental white space—like the visual white space in your living room when you finally clean out all the junk—lets people breathe. *Mental white space helps you breathe.* It's space that inspires rest, calmness, creativity. You can think clearly.

Boredom, free time, and unstructured life is that white space. It gives so many gifts to a child. It inspires creativity and creates space for real friendships. If you're on "bored" (gosh, I couldn't resist), there are a million and one ways to start. I won't pretend to understand the particular inner workings of your home. But to get your wheels turning, here are a few practical suggestions:

- Make a list of all the structured activities your kids do. Draw an X through at least 25 percent of them.
- Spend one Saturday a month being together, just your family, in unscheduled play and rest.
- Foster times when the whole family is intentionally not using technology: rest times, game nights, car rides without devices, Sundays, and so on.
- At the very least, ask yourself this question: How was my childhood different from my kids' childhood, and is this good or bad? Think about that a second. And if this mental

rabbit trail ends up with fond memories of squirting people with rubber bath toys (or the awkward equivalent), don't be afraid to give that same wonderful gift to your kids. Its name is boredom.[1]

Boredom Makes You Create

There are two things I think we did right as young parents. First, we got rid of all the pacifiers before the children turned four. As I type that, it doesn't sound like quite the victory that it was. But at the time it felt like no one in our home would ever have an uninterrupted night of sleep without pacifiers. I was quite sure for a long run that one unnamed child would actually bring it on his honeymoon. But we stuck to our guns, and, future wife, you are welcome!

Another thing I'm glad I did: I continued a daily quiet time after nap time ended. All of my kids were still resting long after they had stopped sleeping in the day. They didn't know anything different. These thirty or so minutes were (are) the bedrock of my day. We all need the time to rest, recalibrate, and recharge.

Truthfully, I needed it most, and I still need it most. By 2:30 p.m. in my day as a homeschool mom, I'm starting to develop an eye twitch and have tense breathing from all the wonderful quality time we've had together. So I guess it started primarily to give us all a break. But one wonderful byproduct of our long-standing rest time has been the creativity that springs up in my kids. This is not a time when we play together. Every single person goes to a different quadrant of the house. There's no one to talk to besides yourself (and some of us do that profusely). There is no technology unless you count the audiobooks and the CD player. This is a mental and physical break.

It started in the first year of their lives when I would let them have time before or after their nap, if they were still contented, to babble and move around in their cribs. My husband and I would laugh hysterically at the sounds our first child made. He loved to hear himself talk (still does!). They'd "read" their books, jump up and down in their cribs, and talk to their stuffed animals.

One time an unnamed child took creative play a step further by "painting" the walls and crib and sheets with poop. That horrific example aside, I find it fascinating what my kids do during this time. The blankness gives a space to imagine and create. I am not saying all my children turn into little geniuses every day. We definitely have those days where I hear, "Mom, can I come down?" every three and a half minutes (not exaggerating). But quite often they will eventually settle into a contented rhythm of quiet and talk, rest and play, and invent these really fascinating projects.

Once my six-year-old came down asking for markers, scissors, and cardboard. I must have been pretty worn down this particular day because I obediently collected the requested supplies and carried them up to the playroom. (P.S. My publisher probably wants me to add that parents should watch their children when they're using scissors. Do as I say, not as I do.) Anyway, my son worked on this project for days in his spare time. He was bursting with pride when he begged me to finally come up and see. Taped to the wall was a nearly life-sized switchboard for the cockpit of an airplane! We'd visited an aviation museum recently, and he had taken what he'd seen and concocted this full-stop aircraft flight-control system with colored-on lights and wheels and buttons. Eventually he even added a brass brad on one piece to make a moveable steering wheel, which I thought was especially ingenious. He was so proud of himself! I was, too, and tried to think more about the creative synapses being formed in his brain and less about what the Scotch tape might be doing to my wall's paint.

A friend of mine shared, "My kids know not to tell me they're bored, or I'll give them jobs! So here they are playing water balloon roulette. They hold the balloon over someone's head and squeeze it until it pops." So there you have it! It's amazing what kids can come up with collectively. One time my boys had the carpet covered with their stuffed animals in a legitimate football formation. I learned it was "animals with legs" versus "animals without legs."

I think it's worth mentioning that if I had given them options of playing *Fortnite* or watching *The LEGO Movie*, they probably would not have said, "Nah, let's go get all our stuffed animals and see if we can remember all the football positions and play a pretend game." Not likely. From which we can conclude two things:

1. Kids need certain atmospheric conditions, so to speak, to get good and bored.
2. Boredom inspires creativity.

Let's begin with number one. What do kids need to enjoy boredom? Because, of course, you can't just constantly leave them in an empty room with no stimulation—that would be inhumane and cruel. Here is what I suggest they must have to make the best of boredom:

- **Stimulation**

    In other words, they need time *not* being bored to enjoy being bored. Otherwise, being bored would be life, and that is no life at all. Though it seems contrary, the first step in giving kids the gift of boredom is giving them the gift of adventure, the kind we discussed in chapter 1. That doesn't mean that you have to take your kid all over creation to play-dates and museums and whatnot. Especially when you have a very young child, there is adventure to be found all over. It could mean that you take a walk across the street and look at the ant hills. Maybe you walk up to the park and swing way up to the sky. Or you dig your feet in the sandbox. At a very desperate moment, I have been known to fill up the bathtub with all the stuffed animals we own to make a sort of dry sensory bath. Honestly, it was a big win.

- **Basic needs**

  If I am hungry, tired, sad, hot, or need to go to the bathroom, and I try to write a book, it will not happen. Likewise, children require their basic needs are met. One study noted that for kids to reach their creative potential, they need to feel safe.[2] It makes sense to me. And I say this to remind all of us that throwing a kid upstairs into a room to have a good time being bored when he's anxious, hungry, or sleep-deprived takes this whole thing out of context.

- **Provisions**

  When you want to bless your kids with the abundance that boredom brings, provisions are necessary. I think there's a time and a place for stripping their room of all the fun stuff. (And that time is when they learn how to crawl out of the crib!) So you'll need to be strategic about what you provide. Maybe it's a fenced-in yard with trucks and sand. Maybe it's a playroom with open-ended toys, like play scarfs, blocks, train tracks, crayons, and LEGOs. Maybe it's a front porch with water and cups and spoons.

A few years ago I got the flu. I feel like you just glossed over that sentence without giving it the weight it deserves. Y'all. This flu was *terrible*. One month in, I thought I was on my literal deathbed. I remember my mom coming to drop off some cranberry juice, and I thought, *Well, Mom, here it is. This is the last time we'll see each other this side of heaven.* By the time it was said and done, I had pneumonia, asthma, the flu, bronchitis, and a stomach bug. As it turns out, I had three little ones who bounced back like it was nothing and still needed clean clothes and their apples sliced and activities to do. One day I got so desperate for rest, I used my last remaining shreds of energy to produce what I called "nap-time kits." I packed up all the interesting things I could garner from around the house. I even included a juice box and a snack. I don't remember the snack, but everyone needs to know that I'm sure it was a safe snack that they wouldn't choke on. Anyway, I made it a real production when I presented their nap-time kits. They were contented for quite some time and actually asked for them for several days afterward! I was investing a little time up front to provide the equipment for being creative in their downtime.

It's often disconcerting to let your kids be bored. The world sometimes screams at us that they should be busy. But if our children's needs have been met, letting them have uninterrupted downtime is a great gift. And this remains true for kids of all ages.

Boredom Builds Friendships

If you do an Internet search for "boredom" and "kids," you will get the distinct impression that these two entities should not co-exist, that kids should never be bored. That explains the Pinterest articles, such as "200 Boredom Busters for Kids" and "25 Ways to Keep Kids Entertained." Well, I call bluff. We've talked about the individual gifts that boredom brings to a developing soul. But there's more! I say letting a slew of kids get good and bored together, without pacifying, distracting, or occupying them, is a profound gift to them all, because it allows real friendships to build.

I am of a generation whose childhood did not have much technology and an adulthood that is inundated with it. I went to college during what was still kind of the technological dark ages. There were few cell phones, except for a few that, get this, you could only use to actually talk to someone. With your voice. Like a weirdo. My dorm rooms all had mounted telephones with cords, so if you wanted to cry to your mom or giggle with a boy you liked, you had to do so sitting on your bed, with your roommate listening. If you wanted to use the Internet, you had to plug an ethernet cable into the wall. As for e-mail, once a day I would get a message from the Dean of Something-or-Other, but it was never very interesting and you already kind of knew the information anyway.

The only *fun* social media that existed was IM, or instant messenger. For those youngsters who don't know, this was a not-so-glorified way to mass text, but, again, it only worked from a plugged-in computer, so you had to be sitting in your room to use it. If you were out, you could leave an "away message" that could cryptically or not-so-cryptically tell everyone where you were or the state of your soul. I was really good at crafting these away messages, by the way. One I remember was "It's like wringing water from a dry washcloth." I have no idea what it meant, but doesn't it sound gripping? Anyway, the key part of this whole system was, to use it, you had to be next to your computer, which had to be plugged into the wall. In other words, when you were out with your friends, you were *with* your friends.

I wish I could go back to this college life for just one day. Not for my good looks because College Jessica had an abnormal fixation on mock turtlenecks and unflattering ankle-length khaki skirts. And not for the food because, aside from Chicken Tender Night, I honestly don't know how we even ate the nonsense they served to us as dinner. Not for all that but for the freedom we had to enjoy friendship, undistracted.

Yesterday I passed eight kids waiting for the middle school bus. Every single one of them was completely absorbed in his or her phone. These kids were passing this "boring" moment waiting at a stoplight by entertaining themselves with scrolling apps or playing games. Because I have a weird brain, I always see things like this and think to myself, *I wonder what these kids would be doing if they weren't on their phones.* Would they be making jokes? Talking about the Panthers game? Chatting with our neighbor, Miss Toni, about the new terrier she just adopted from the rescue center? Playing UNO? Reading *Calvin and Hobbes*?

We've forgotten that friends - technology = a profound gift.

I know this is true for two reasons.

First, statistics prove it. Loneliness, depression, and anxiety are skyrocketing in the uber-busy, highly connected generation.[3] Our teenagers are highly entertained and occupied but deeply unfulfilled. Our kids are telling us over and over again that they are lonely, that there is a friendship deficit.

Second, you can see it anecdotally. A friend of mine shared her insights after chaperoning an eighth-grade overnight field trip. The first day, all devices were confiscated. As you may imagine, there was weeping and withdrawal. The kids had no idea how to function. They asked repeatedly to be given back their phones for this or that reason, to the point that they were actually threatened with a severe consequence if anyone asked again! The chaperones did allow the kids to have their phones for ten minutes at the end of each day, in which they could check in with parents, keep their "Snapchat streams" active, whatever. My friend observed that on the first day most students retrieved their phones for the allowed period. The second day, she noted, only about ten students wanted the phones. On the third day, maybe one or two did. On the way home the kids begged, "No! Don't give us back our phones! It's way more fun without them!"[4]

I think this incident is incredibly telling. And also sad. When you get rid of boredom, one casualty is friendship. A lot of stuff, meaningful stuff, happens in that unplanned, unfilled downtime.

I will go a step further and say I really don't think you can be a good friend without learning to be comfortable with boredom. Here is why: to be a true friend requires patience. It requires the ability to listen through a long story, to troubleshoot a problem that is not yours, to push through something you don't feel like doing because someone you love does enjoy it. I agree that technology is incredible. In under a minute, we can order a chicken sandwich, stream a movie, or chat with a doctor. But we must not forget that patience is a gift, because no true friendship exists without it.

So what do we do with this? We live in an age with so many activities and so much technology. How do we raise kids that know how to have friends, and to be friends, in this age? I am not suggesting that we need to adopt an Amish lifestyle to have friendships; that would be silly. But we will need to make decisions, some of them hard ones, about how we spend our time.

There is one wonderful step we can take, and that is to put screens away when we're spending time with one another. If your kids are having a party, collect all the devices at the door. If the neighbor kids are playing together, make them ride bikes or make cookies instead of watching TV or playing video games. And if you're playing a game as a family, put the devices away. If you go out to dinner, put the phones away. If you're on a long car trip, I repeat, put the phones away. Be bored together! It's painful and annoying and absolutely precious.

Right now my husband and I are the only ones in our family with phones, but it is really convicting to think about the example we are setting. If we want our kids to be people who cherish people, then we need to set that example. As is so often the case, being authentic in parenting is devastatingly important.

All the Things Your Kid Misses While on a Device at a Sibling's Sporting Event

I'm going to begin with a preface: I have two older boys who play sports and a daughter who does not yet play sports. Which is to say, we spend a lot of time on baseball fields and basketball courts. And the result is that I have a five-year-old daughter who has lived large segments of her life literally on the sidelines. She's really a trouper and has accumulated about as much knowledge of the rules of baseball as I have as a grown woman (which admittedly is not much).

But, y'all, it's hard. Sometimes it's fun, and we jump on the bleachers and play with friends and watch the setting sun on the horizon, and an hour breezes by like nothing. But sometimes, not so much. Instead she'll be sweaty, whiny, exhausted, climbing on my lap, and really should have been in bed an hour ago. When I look at the time and see that a whole seventeen minutes have elapsed of a ninety-minute practice, I might feel a little desperate and allow her to look at pictures on my phone. She thinks this is the pinnacle of entertainment. She told me one time with fierceness, "When I get to be a mom, I'm going to look at pictures on my phone for the whole, entire day!" I was not quite sure how to reply to this threat.

All this is to say, I do believe that things can escalate to that point of desperation, where the modern mother can freely use the tools afforded her as a member of the technology generation. But I believe those times should be few and far between. I believe that we shouldn't toss our kids a screen at the slightest inkling of boredom or discontentment. (Important ancillary point: neither should we, as adults, gravitate to our own screens in the same angsty moments.)

And why not? This is a valid question. After all, screens make you feel better right away. They shut kids up, immediately. So why in the world should any adult make their own lives harder and more frequently interrupted by needy, whiny kids? As I said, it's a valid question, but I believe the answer is absolutely clear. While an iPhone does make our own lives and our kids' lives *immediately* better, it is robbing us in the long run of something meaningful. "Robbing." I know, a strong word for streaming a few YouTube videos. But I believe it is accurate in light of what can instead be gained from these snippets of time.

The last baseball game we attended, a boy who looked to be about eight crouched under the bleachers on an iPhone, pecking and swiping, totally engrossed for the two-hour event. He barely looked up long enough to eat one of the Goldfish crackers in the bag next to him. It broke my heart. Somewhere on the field in front of him was a sibling. Someone to watch, to root for. Somewhere nearby was a grown-up who, presumably, loved him and could have spent time with him. Please understand that I am not passing judgment on this particular scenario. I don't know this child; he could have severe special needs. I don't know these parents; perhaps they had just suffered a tremendous loss and even showing up to this game was a costly effort. But I cannot help but contrast what this boy was experiencing with what *could* have been. When our kids are involved in an event, we can be there or we can *be there*.

Want to know a few things your kids are missing out on if they're on devices at a sporting event?

- **They miss cheering for a sibling.** Don't we want our kids to be the kind who cheer one another on? This training starts now. What are we teaching kids when we bring them to events and hand them devices? We are teaching them that being entertained is more important than encouraging a friend. Now, listen. I'm not sitting at every single practice applauding every little swing, lap, or kick. That would be tremendous overkill and would feed the monster of your child's ego. But when it really matters, and something is happening on a field or court or stage or wherever it is, then the family should pay attention. The very youngest can learn this. My two-year-old niece, Logan, and I were cheering together at the soccer game this morning. You better believe she loved to clap and scream when her brother had the ball!

- **They miss making friends.** When I was in seventh grade, my friend Angela and I both had brothers who practiced soccer on Tuesday nights at 7:00 p.m. We had the absolute best time during practice. We would run up and down the big hill outside the school. We'd lie on our backs in the grass and daydream about what our favorite teacher/crush Mr. Gann was doing right then. We would tell stories and jokes and eat bubble gum her mom had in her purse. Because I was a timid, reserved little thing in a brand-new school, this snatch of time each week became my favorite time to spend with my hilarious friend Angela. We forged a real friendship because, well, what else did we really have to do?

- **They miss out on enjoying nature.** Perhaps this one sounds cliche, but studies have proven again and again the effects of nature on child development.[5] If your event is outdoors, this is an ideal time to soak up the chance to be outside. To notice the clouds and trees, put bare feet in the grass, collect weeds, watch the moon come out on the other side of the sky. All sorts of therapy happens thanks to nature.

- **They miss engaging with grown-ups.** My son has developed a friendship with one of the parents on his brother's team. They'll play catch off to the side, throw long bombs, chat about his upcoming games or the book he's reading. This engagement is so precious, and it would never have happened if my son had the option to be sucked into a screen. I guarantee you he'd not be hanging out with this thirty-year-old dad if he had the chance to be on a screen, but what a gift it's been.

- **They miss unstructured, interactive play.** So much of childhood play is structured by adults. Time to play freely is a rare and valuable gift. The ability to go free and play tag on an open field, throw rocks down a sewage drain, balance on the beams of wood down the sidewalk, sit with a mound of crayons and a favorite coloring book or a sack of beads and a string. What a gift we give our kids with an hour to themselves!

- **They miss learning the skill of patience.** Patience is crucial to adulthood success. Patient grown-ups are faithful to their spouses. Patient grown-ups don't scream at their kids (well, you know . . . mostly). Patient grown-ups don't explode with road rage or angrily bark orders to the Starbucks barista. We want the byproducts of patience for our world and our children, but it costs something; it is a skill that needs developing. What a gift! At a sporting event you have an entire hour to hone this skill!

- **They miss out on spending time with you.** A few years ago, I saw an image on Instagram that I have not forgotten. It showed a jar of marbles—936 marbles, to be exact. Next to this jar was another one about half full. Each of the marbles, the caption explained, stood for one weekend you had with your kid before he leaves your home. That second, half-full jar (with 572 marbles) represented how many you had left if you had a seven-year-old. It was a sobering image. We sometimes feel that parenthood drags along mercilessly—that we will forever be making bottles or chicken nuggets or everyone hush up in the car. In fact, the reality is that these years are limited, and as my mom says, they begin snowballing after your kids start kindergarten, racing past you faster and faster until they're gone in what feels like a blink of time. There are no magic moments that are more special than others. It all counts. How often have I heard an older friend say, "I miss the days when I had all this time with my kids. Now they are teenagers, and they're never home." Dear mom who is exhausted and enduring yet another long day, these years will not last. One little game of Candy Land will probably not kill you. (Although I have definitely felt that "death by too many Candy Land games" would be on my tombstone.)

And, P.S., this goes for us parents too. Quality time with the kids, enjoying nature, growing patience, cheering for family, making friends—we also miss all of these when we keep checking on this or that. And we can add one more thing to our list: the chance to show our kids what kind of adults to be.

CHAPTER FOUR

THE GIFT OF BEING UNCOOL

How and Why to Let Your

Kids Be Awkward

About a year ago my nine-year-old son said to me, "Mom, I don't really enjoy LEGOs anymore. They're not really fun." I wept inside remembering the mornings he'd be camped out at the kitchen table reading the instructions for his kits from Nanna or proudly designing his own LEGO creations—like a submarine grocery store or a jail for bad sharks. I didn't expect it to end this early.

I didn't say anything in response or immediately begin packing them all up. Surely he couldn't mean it.

Fast-forward one year. I started again hearing LEGO sounds coming from the upstairs. There was also LEGO talk. And when my boys went to play with the neighbors, they were balancing their creations in their arms, carrying them to go outside. LEGOs had made a comeback. I didn't even mind when I would step on a misplaced four-prong square in the dark and experience that sharp pain as if the nerves in my foot were getting electrocuted. That's a lie. I did mind that part.

But it was worth it.

As I write these words, an entire LEGO kingdom has sprung into existence. And honestly, it's the oldest kids that are the most passionate. An entire elaborate and complicated LEGO civilization exists with rules and currency that somehow everyone understands and remembers. From what I've gathered, every LEGO accessory has some monetary value. A piece of cheese, for example, is worth fifty gold "LEGO moneys." (This is a lot of money in LEGO world. Cheese is very valuable.) There are all sorts of complex laws. If your LEGO guy falls off the table, he's dead. If he's riding a certain hoverboard, he's not dead. If he was shoved maliciously off the table by another player, that player owes you one hundred LEGO moneys. This rule has recently come under controversy, as there have been a lot of accidental deaths of LEGO guys who were simply in the wrong place at the wrong time.

The kids transport their LEGOs around the neighborhood in various contraptions. My kids use small tackle boxes to house their guys and all their parts. Come to think of it, I'm not sure whether these tackle boxes have ever been used for fishing equipment, but nothing smells like fish, so I'm letting it slide. Two neighbor boys store their entire LEGO collections in pillowcases, so when they're traveling, they look like they're channeling their inner Santa. The amazing thing to me is that ten kids will congregate in one garage, dump everything out so the floor looks like a LEGO piñata has exploded, and still somehow they remember *exactly* whose minuscule piece is whose. It is honestly impressive.

My brother-in-law has coined the phrase the "League of Dorks" to describe the hilarious, creative, imaginative play that our young boys have come up with. The League of Dorks has also done a book club on a few Harry Potter titles, opened up the paper-snake-selling store I mentioned earlier, and enjoyed Star Wars movie nights. The League of Dorks is said tongue in cheek and with such endearment. We laugh at their LEGO villages, but secretly we're thrilled, and we're proud. They have no speck of self-consciousness, no concern on meeting a "coolness" standard. These kids are *being kids*.

The thing is, LEGO civilization is precisely the kind of playing that ten-year-old boys should be doing. Ten-year-old boys should not be rating girls on the Hot or Not app (or the next-gen equivalent that is current when you are reading this). They should not be scrolling semipornographic Instagram accounts or laughing at adult comedians on YouTube. They should be free to play in an age-appropriate way.

Unadulterated play is a little ecosystem that is beautiful to observe, but there are external forces that could forever destroy it. I have thought about this a lot. It's not always bad; growing up happens. Nature takes its course. The LEGOs end up on Facebook Marketplace or on a forgotten shelf in a teenager's room. But sometimes innocent play dies an unnatural death that disrupts the rightful course of childhood. How does this happen? Why do kids stop playing?

- **They get made fun of.** Imagine if an older kid walked into a garage with a LEGO village and cruelly mocked it, saying, "Wow. This is the lamest thing I've ever seen. Are you guys seriously playing with toys? This is hilarious." You may have a few who shrug it off, but after a while the spell is broken, and LEGOs aren't cool.
- **They can't focus.** It is a type of work for kids to engage in interactive, creative play. It takes practice and mental capacity.

Someone who's been passively entertained by high-tech, digitally enhanced entertainment for seven to eight hours a day will have little patience for conversational, two-dimensional, innovative play with plastic manipulatives.[1]

- **Adults poke fun at them.** This mocking can come intentionally or unintentionally. We can also make them feel like they're stupid, roll our eyes at their play and their little games. We must respect childhood and respect play. Back to my League of Dorks example. The first time this phrase was said in earshot of one of the kids, he didn't understand it but also didn't like it. That's when one of the uncles worked hard to turn it around by creating a cool club with benefits. The League of Dorks became a household name, a highly desired monthly occurrence.

We need to value our kids' play. It's worth our money and our respect. As I type this, there are a bunch of kids (and a few moms) in the cul-de-sac of my neighborhood. Some are on bikes, some are on scooters, some are pushing baby strollers, and a few are off to the side throwing a football. Then there are the boys inside a garage trading (you guessed it) LEGOs. This time LEGO heads for LEGO wheels. At first glance it seems organic and unforced. But quite a few things had to happen for the kids and scooters to be happily coexisting on a random Thursday:

- **We had to be home.** Saying yes to organic play means that you sometimes say no. We don't do every club or lesson or errand that we could, because being home to play freely matters.
- **We had to be outside.** I don't think I need to beat this dead horse, but if it's beautiful outside, can't we all be in agreement to *send the kids outside*?

- **No one is making fun of them.** In our world, children are respected. Their innocent play is respected. We don't tolerate big kids making fun of little kids simply for being little kids.

Kids today face an unfathomable pressure to be "cool." What a wonderfully kind gift to release them from this burden. In the following essays I'll talk about how to give the gift of authenticity to our kids. One way we do this is by replacing nonstop peer time with friendship with grown-ups. Another is by carving out space for the awkward years (so necessary for healthy development). And finally, we let them play like kids play—with LEGO kingdoms and dressed-up bunnies and too-tight Batman costumes—for just as long as they need to.

Fewer Peers, More
Intergenerational Relationships

One of my favorite people growing up was my aunt Rebecca. Aunt Rebecca was, as we termed her, "one of the fun moms." This didn't have anything to do with her clothes being on point (they weren't) or whether or not she had a pulse on what was cool in pop culture (she didn't). She was one of the fun moms because she had time for us. When she finished her morning chores, she'd take us horseback riding on one of the old standardbreds that lived on their Maryland horse farm. She would also take us with her when she went to the vitamin store or the large-animal feed store, chatting the whole time. You got the feeling she told you stuff the other moms wouldn't tell you. Things like how horses act before they're about to mate, what Uncle Tommy did with the bloody parts of the deer when he was done skinning it, and what she really thought of her brother's first wife.

One summer when it was time to say goodbye to Aunt Rebecca, because we had to return to city life and our school routines, I remember leaving her house, walking past the strawberry plants and the old water pump, with a heavy sadness in my chest. "One thing I'm really going to miss," my cousin Kelly said, "is Aunt Rebecca." I couldn't answer without crying. Later I wrote her a real card and mailed it. I told her I missed her. "Even though your house isn't always the cleanest," I said, "it is one of my favorite places to visit." She, of course, took that as the compliment it was, and the card hung on her fridge for at least two years.

I think one of the tragedies of our times is how everyone is segmented according to how old they are. Schools, churches, gyms—whenever people tend to gather, they're grouped according to age. This is to everyone's detriment.

I remember in college, where we were lumped together with

other near-adults our same age, that we mourned the loss of "babies and dogs and old people," those individuals and animals that we no longer had interaction with. Childhood, like early adulthood, is made richer by doing life with those who are not exactly our same age—those babies and old people and, of course, our pets.

Three years ago my grandmother moved from four states away into my parents' house. This has been a long act of kindness and self-sacrifice for my parents. I have learned more about loving others by the way they—primarily my mother—have willingly shouldered this responsibility than I have learned in the past thirty-seven years combined. I honestly wasn't sure I'd ever see Grammy again, but now we have the opportunity to care for her after she has cared for all of us her whole life. Another peripheral blessing has been the opportunity for our own children to love and be loved by Grammy. My preschool daughter loves to help care for Great-Grammy. *"Help! Great-Grammy is getting out of her chair by herself!"* she'll alert us with full force. They're great friends, actually, with a plethora of shared hobbies: coloring, puzzles, Pepsi, and doughnuts. I hope that it never feels unusual for my daughter to have a dear friend who is ninety-one years old.

It's wonderful and sweet, but at the root is something very true and powerful: there is no substitute for how intergenerational relationships bless our children. So what do intergenerational relationships offer us?

- **They offer perspective.**

    When I was about twelve years old, school got hard. Not math and science, but being around kids who suddenly cared where your clothes were from and if you listened to KISS 95.1 FM or not. I remember my mom crept in my room one night. She said, "Jessica, some people are like fireworks. They're bright and showy and everyone loves them right away. Some people, though, are like candles. You don't notice them right away but they're just as special, just as wonderful." I got the point; I was a candle.

Seventh grade can be oppressive and exhausting. Grown-ups are a welcome relief because it doesn't matter that they're not cool; actually, that is precisely the relief. When I hung out with Aunt Rebecca, she was deliciously different from the eleven-year-olds I was with all day long. And that in and of itself was a reality check. What I felt during school wasn't the only thing that was real. There was a whole big world outside of that. I was loved, I was accepted, and one day I would have a real future that didn't involve dumb sixth-grade boys.

When my sister was in eighth grade, my mom pulled her out of school to homeschool her. If you ask Mom today why she did this, she won't mention math skills or improved SAT prep. It had little to do with academics. I think there were some warning signs that she was about to hit a rough patch. She was already beautiful, but she'd gotten into this technique of applying makeup so that her entire face was dramatically ashen white, except for half a tube of black eyeliner around the eyes. The eighth-grade boys were nearly knocking the door down.

My parents were about as excited about the raccoon-eye-makeup situation as they were about the boys knocking down the door. I think my mom felt like she'd tried about everything to connect with my sister without much luck. So homeschool for eighth grade it was. Between you and me, I don't think they did much of what you could technically call school. I think they baked a lot of cookies, went to the gym and coffee shops, ate lunch together, and read their Bibles. I'm not setting up this situation as the pinnacle of academic achievement, but I personally think it was a brilliant plan. My sister got a reality check, time with my mom, and a real-life (and face) makeover. It was a year to right the ship. It showed my sister that there was, in fact, a wonderful life outside of dating eighth-grade punks. We are all grateful she snapped out of it and didn't end up with any of them. This is how being around quality grown-ups is a life preserver for kids.

- **They offer opportunities for authentic friendship with wonderful people.**

  The notion that you have to be the same age to be friends is mind-boggling to me. My Pop-Pop and I loved Garfield books and word searches and potato perogies. My little niece Katie loves to take bike rides, and sometimes we will do a lap, just the two of us. My friend says her son genuinely loves spending time with an eighty-year-old neighbor who has all sorts of interesting stories about wartime, spaceships, and astronomy. Her son will beg, "Can I *please* go talk to Mrs. Wilson now?" Age brings depth, wisdom, and interest. If we group our kids with only little humans exactly like them, they're missing a whole captivating world of knowledge, wisdom, kindness, and character. Let's give them grown-ups for friends.

- **They teach you about death.**

  (Yes, this is a good thing.) Ben Sasse comments, "In our age-segregated era, we spend enormous energy, time, and money letting the young and middle-aged pretend eternal youth is attainable, rather than actually grappling with the inevitable, and rather than comforting those actually declining."[2] I find this insight profound and convicting. I so sympathize with this tendency. I loathe nursing homes, because I loathe thinking about myself getting old. But in avoiding them (and avoiding older adults), I rob myself of an examined life and of the chance to comfort those who are growing old. And the same goes for our children.

What would it look like for your family to become richer with intergenerational friendships? How could your children be comforted, challenged, and blessed by older grown-ups who love them? Consider who you might add to your circle of influence, and then invite them to join you sometime.

Let's Revive the Awkward Years

When my daughter was three, we enrolled her in dance. She loved it and looked absolutely adorable in her little toddler tutu. The only little hiccup came at the end of the year when it was time for the very official dance studio recital.

First, the toddler girls had to purchase an outfit that for sure cost as much as the dress I wore to my wedding rehearsal dinner. Then we got instructions for the recital that seemed oddly reminiscent of a professional dance studio performance:

- Drop dancers off one hour beforehand. Dancers must be in full hair, makeup, and costume, and then parents are to leave. (Under no circumstances can parents be backstage before the ~~Miss America Pageant~~ Toddler Dance Recital.)
- Professional hair updos are not required but *highly* recommended. Professional makeup artist provided on-site for a small fee.
- Review attached pictures for your *exact* hairstyle: bun pigtails, low ponytail (left side part only!), high bun, tilting to the left side, feathers facing east, use Aussie freeze hair spray only! *Don't mess it up!*
- Makeup required. Fake eyelashes suggested. Blush mandatory. Gobs and gobs of lipstick and nail polish and glitter eyeshadow and feathers and just everything.

Now, look, I am not on a rant against girls taking dance. Our daughter still dances (although at a different studio, one more *Nutcracker*, less *America's Next Top Model*). And I am certainly not against little girls wanting to be pretty. I love dressing my little sunshine up, and she loves it too. She loves to wear her "swirly dress" and do twirls around the living room. Being pretty is a natural desire for little girls. It's just that somehow the deadline for being on-trend and glamorous got pushed from "when it's your wedding" to "when you attend a school of any kind, including preschool."

You know what it was like when I was a kid? When I turned ten (ten!), my cousin and I got to go to the mall to get a new shirt. Our choices were basically pink with hearts or purple with hearts. I got the pink; she got the purple. (Important note: *we were thrilled*.)

If I browse the clothing section of a popular store for girls, for example, Forever 21, I begin to feel really insecure about my own wardrobe as a thirty-seven-year-old woman. I mean, how do I not have a striped jumper, a "houndstooth skater dress," or a faux suede moto jacket? Of course, if our preteen friends are feeling more casual, they can grab a graphic t-shirt with a message, such as "Spoiled," "My Unicorn Ate My Homework," "I'm So Bored," "AC/DC," or "Whatever." Not just high schoolers but now preteen girls are mastering contoured makeup and the smoky eye, purchasing thongs, debating bikini waxes, and refilling gel manicures. None of this is an exaggeration. These things are actually happening.

What has happened to the awkward years? Seriously, what in the world happened to them? They have died and been buried eight feet deep. I think Brittany Spears killed them. Want to know what I was doing as a preteen girl? I guarantee you it had nothing to do with contouring or houndstooth skater dresses.

First of all, I was terribly awkward. I had large turquoise-colored wire-rimmed glasses, a cowlick the size of Kentucky, and buckteeth that I had absolutely no conscious awareness of. Don't worry, by seventh grade I'd gotten it figured out. Except that is a joke . . . I did *not* have it figured out. It was even worse than before because the glasses had turned to tortoiseshell, my favorite outfit involved an oversized, faded NASCAR t-shirt of my favorite driver, and then you can add emerging teenage acne into the picture. I had no magical Disney-movie experience where I realized how awkwardly uncool I was and became transformed by a much cooler, and surprisingly nicer, friend I met on the cheerleading squad. That did not happen. And hey, you there reading, don't act like I'm some anomaly. You have these pictures, too, I know it!

I've been talking about girls in particular, but this concept applies to both genders today. Boys, too, are expected to be cool from an early age. In addition to having to wear the "right" sneakers and brands of t-shirts, they are expected to know the right songs, get the right jokes, watch the right shows, and play the right games. A friend told me his kid said, "Dad, when I tell my friends what my score is in *Fortnite*, they all make fun of me!" His dad kindly reminded him that he is more than his *Fortnite* score and not to worry for two seconds about these "friends." Kids these days feel a pressure we parents cannot understand to be "someone" and to look like it too.

I submit to you that with the death—nay, the *murder*—of the Awkward Years, we have lost something beautiful for our children.[3]

If you want to give your kids a real gift, give them the freedom to be awkward. Guard them from ridiculous expectations. Let them meander awkwardly into adulthood. But how? How exactly does one impart this gift to their kids? I have three suggestions.

1. **Realize your kids are not you.**

    Work it out in your head that your kids aren't a reflection of your own coolness or togetherness, and let them be who they are. Don't ever allow them to have the power to embarrass you. You are you and they are them. This isn't easy. It feels good when people tell you that your kids are cute or funny or nice or great at sports, and you can't unfeel the internal satisfaction those comments bring. So it can be a bit of a fight to hold it loosely. Don't bolster yourself or rely on affirmation. Yes, that's the best way to say it; hold it very loosely.

Your kids are their own little beings. What a tremendous gift you give them to mature and grow freely without you hovering above them at all junctures hoping they're turning out to be specimens pleasing to everyone everywhere. My friend Jessica is one of the coolest people I know and legit looks like a supermodel. Yet I love how she lets her five kids be perfectly themselves, even if it means they do *not* always look like mini versions of her, aka mini supermodels. Jess says, "The kids I've been given are like surprise packages. I can't *wait* to see who they will become. Life's a journey. So I encourage them as they emerge individually. Be nerdy, be awkward, be accidentally trendy, but please, above all, be *you*!"[4] Amen!

2. **Don't be afraid to go against the current.**

In love, shelter your kids from anything or anyone that will pressure them to be something they aren't. I know the word *shelter* often has negative connotations, as if to shelter kids from the real world is overreactive, irrelevant, and harkening to a more puritan society. I say there is a time and a place for a shelter. If you were plopped on a forsaken island, you'd long for a shelter from dangerous elements. We offer our children the kind gift of a comforting shelter—not just a physical one in our cozy homes but a figurative one, which protects childhood.

You know that feeling you get when you scroll through Instagram and feel ugly, friendless, uncool, unsuccessful, and miserable? Give your kids the gift of a childhood without that feeling. That means you wield your adult-sized power and control to shelter them (I know, I know—that word again) from stuff that tends to trigger that ickiness. We want to gift our children with the ability to be authentic. That means when you are eight years old, you act like you are eight—not thirteen. My goodness, this a difficult job. But it's not impossible.

It's hard to predict what specific steps this may mean for your family in your culture. But my guess is, for me, living this message will eventually involve the following: spending next to no time on that vehicle of self-comparison, aka social media; limiting the time we spend with anything geared to teenagers such as Claire's, the Target teen section, and all the other preteen stores that will spring into existence after the writing of this book; and not letting the youngest ones in the house do and see everything the oldest ones can do and see. You are the grown-up and you are wise. Use your power and influence as a parent to allow age-appropriate activities that will be a positive influence. Go with your gut.

3. **And, maybe most importantly, speak love and like and confidence into your kids. They so desperately need it.**

I taught seventh-grade English literature, and in my class was a girl we'll call Madison. She was as awkward and gangly as they come. Crooked smile hinting at impending braces. Acne and frizzy hair. Skinny as a rail. What struck me as a pleasant surprise was Madison's confidence. She didn't seem bothered by her awkward legs or funny smile. She would breeze in the door, smiling at everyone, and run to tell me of her recent dance competition or family vacation. She had a little group of friends and happily did all the silly things that seventh-grade girls did in Christian schools before social media was everything.

One day Madison's daddy came into class. Oh, did she beam. And so did he! He was bringing flowers for her birthday. A well-dressed, nice-looking man, he headed straight for his sweetheart with brownies and red roses. Madison was in heaven! And suddenly, it all made sense. Her confidence was because she knew she was loved. As I watched her grow up, the awkward smile and acne disappeared. She reached out to me a few years ago to tell me how much she had loved having me for a teacher and to catch me up on her plans for her life. What a gift she had: a father who thought she was the most precious thing ever! She became what he told her she was.

I am not saying it will be easy, but allowing an awkward, meandering, growing-up time is one of the kindest things we can do for our children. After all, what a tremendous gift—freedom to be just who you are. Let them be kids. Let them be awkward.

Let Them Have Stuffed Animals

Even though it makes my blood pressure rise, I like to keep abreast of the stuff that stores are marketing to kids. Recently I browsed the website of a store that sells accessories to young girls. Let's take a minute and recognize that girls who are seven, eight, and nine years old are frequenting this store. Here are a few things I saw:

- Gothic temporary tattoos
- a pleather "Halloween devil" costume
- an "evil witch" outfit with a corset and miniskirt
- a marble iPhone case with a flip mirror to "check your makeup"
- faux nails and body glitter

Goodness gracious, I was a literal *baby* compared to all this. I absolutely would not have known what to do with leopard-print nails or body glitter. At the risk of sounding like a complete weirdo, can I tell you what I was doing when I was six or seven? I spent most of my days with my friends "Lambsley" and "Blanketsly," who were stuffed animals. Lambsley had at one point been a plush and fluffy lamb, but unfortunately his stuffing kept leaking out. Mom scraped out the rest and deemed him a puppet. I don't remember that being as traumatic as it sounds. Blanketsly was so well used that he began shredding at the ends as childhood blankets tend to do. Mom, to the rescue again, sewed him into a sort of pillow creature.

Every few months Lambsley and Blanketsly reached that point of stuffed animal grossness that required a good washing. This was a devastating loss on two counts. For one, I'd worked really hard to get them smelling that perfect way a beloved stuffed thing does. And second, it meant that for a torturous three hours Lambsley and Blanketsly were, for all intents and purposes, gone. I would sit on the cold cement floor in the basement by the dryer and sob until I could hug them again and resume our tea party. I had no language for tattoos and dressing up like a sexy witch.

Don't get me wrong. I understand that little girls are drawn like magnets to unicorns and dress-up and sparkly, shiny things. I have a daughter, and I have no doubt she could spend $500 in that formerly mentioned store if she were left to her own devices. We have the rest of our lives, however, to wear blue mascara and faux nails, but only *a few brief years* in which to cuddle a sheep puppet.

Why rush everything?

Let's go back for a second to those hours I spent crying for my stuffed things in front of the dryer. I'm going to make a statement that will seem totally crazy: *those moments* are just as important as any time I could have spent practicing to be a teenager, in a pre-school classroom, or at a STEM-based summer camp. Yes, playing with stuffed animals is *doing something* for a young child, even though it looks like nothing.

Stuffed animals are important to childhood. And I will prove it.

I'm generally not one to toot my own horn but—*toot*—I'm breaking my rule for a minute. You see that girl sobbing by the dryer over a polyester puppet? She grew up to be the Homecoming Queen, gives speeches at conferences, and loves meeting strangers at parties. I did just fine, thank you very much. And I'm fine, not *despite* the hours spent cuddling my stuffed animals but *because* of them. I warned you—it sounds crazy. But I firmly believe it. I am healthy because I had the time and space to be a kid. There were plenty of stretching moments, but they came along at a slow and manageable pace.

Yes, I've thought about it a lot, and I think a stuffed animal friend is essential to a good childhood. (I use "stuffed animal" loosely; one little boy faithfully brings his beloved green Matchbox truck to the Sunday school class I teach every week.)

An aunt of ours bought matching plush dachshunds for me and my cousin Rebecca. One summer the stuffed dachshunds (both named Darla) traveled to Washington, DC. On the evening of day two, the most exciting thing that could have happened, happened. We were on the fifth floor of the Marriott when the fire alarm went off. Being in a hotel was already next-level thrilling, and now this? Rebecca and I each grabbed our respective Darlas and raced down the stairs to escape the danger. We have pictures of the dachshunds held up triumphantly next to the ~~burning~~ building where someone pulled the alarm. Her Darla would often write letters and postcards to my Darla, who wasn't quite as faithful in her letter-writing habits but nevertheless enjoyed getting them. I think it is important to tell you that we were near middle school before these letters started to fizzle. I guess we should have been embarrassed about such childish activity, but no one bothered to tell us that. (Rebecca really struggled, like I did. She only grew up to be a private-practice attorney.)

With these kinds of memories, I have a tender spot in my heart for the times I'm vacuuming and come upon my daughter's Bunny in a stroller, diapered and tenderly tucked in. I remember the Christmas I let the boys have their own little Christmas tree in their room. One night I came up to see Banjo, the stuffed dog, lying next to the tree with his blanket and pillow. Who wouldn't enjoy sleeping underneath the Christmas tree?

Of course, this whole thing is a blessing and a curse, as any parent knows who has made prayerful laps around the house at bedtime looking for Mr. Pickles or Brown Bear. I had my first initiation into this club when someone gifted Samule the Mule to my son. Samule earned his Velveteen status in an impressive year and a half. There are only three strands of black horsey hair left on his tail because my son rubbed his tail between his two chubby fingers to fall asleep every night. Samule the Mule has gone golfing, swimming, has pooped on the potty, buried his toes in the sand, received albuterol through the nebulizer, been thrown up on, covered in poop, has eaten oatmeal, gotten his hair dried, helped to make Jesus' birthday cake, and, needless to say, been through more cycles of the washing machine than anything with stuffing should. Around month six of his very active life, Todd and I came to the firm conclusion that we would all go to sleep much easier if there were a backup Samule on hand.

Here is where we went wrong. First, I ordered a mini Samule, accidentally. Who reads the fine print of dimensions on stuffed animal orders anyway? I am embarrassed to admit I thought it might make do in case of an emergency. Rookie mistake. When my son saw mini Samule, he literally laughed out loud. We were dirt poor, and I wasn't about to spend nineteen dollars for a toddler joke. Mini Samule was promptly returned.

Then backup Samule arrived in the correct dimensions. This is when it became obvious exactly how loved (read: disgusting) the real Samule had become. He was truly a shadow of his former self, so the new Samule was also promptly identified as an imposter. We tried to use him once as a backup, and my son called him Comfortable Samule, repeatedly asking for Real Samule. I know what you're thinking, but all attempts to make him look disheveled have failed. No matter how many times I stomped on or washed him, somehow Comfortable Samule came out looking fluffier and more comfortable, and Real Samule rattier and more gnarled. Apparently there is no substitute for the loving, snotty, sweaty hands of a two-year-old. There was more than one evening where Velveteen Samule was missing, and two adults—two full-grown, exhausted, busy adults—searched obediently for twenty-five minutes for a ten-inch stuffed mule while our toddler moaned for him in his crib, imposter Samule in hand. It sounds funny, but at the time it sure was not. (PSA for new parents who want to do this right: my brother-in-law bought six pink elephants from the get-go, all of whom are named Trunkers, and all of whom constantly rotate through naps and bedtime. Expensive but brilliant.)[5]

I remember when I was packing for college and my dad came up to my room. "Are you bringing Lambsley and Blanketsly with you?" he asked with a sweet, sad smile. I mumbled something like, "I guess so," and then hid them under my pillows for the first semester. Poor Dad. I think I now know how he felt. A few nights ago I was cleaning up after all the kids were in bed, and I found Samule, not the fake one but the real one, thrown carelessly on the stairs. He wasn't needed anymore. Part of me was really sad, but I picked him up and felt grateful for the part he played in my son's childhood. I walked him upstairs and laid him on my now-ten-year-old's bed (you know, just in case).

You don't make kids play with stuffed animals. It is more a matter of providing materials (soft and friendly-looking friends), providing time (not rushing everywhere the whole day long), and, most of all, providing an unhurried spirit (letting childhood be childhood). You buy the stuffed mule or dog or doll or whatever. You aren't constantly rushing them to more "important" things. You don't make them feel silly when they need Mr. Pickles to fall asleep or come on vacation. Maybe you wait just a bit longer before you go in those older stores or hang with those older friends. And you let them be a little awkward, maybe even uncool, and hang on to those childhood toys and stuffed animal a little longer.

Even if it means that you end up with a flashlight on the neighbor's trampoline, hunting for a gray bunny with a zipping pouch on his bottom. Not that I've been there, but you know . . . hypothetically.

CHAPTER FIVE

THE GIFT OF IMAGINATION

Creative Play, Saving Reading, and
A Family Technology Manifesto

One night my dad picked me up from my evening piano lessons. His face was beaming as he said, "I've got something for you."

My little brother John nearly exploded from the station wagon. "Dad has a surprise for you. You're going to love it so much! It's what you've always wanted." There were plastic bags from the local grocery store two layers thick on the floor of the car. I couldn't imagine what they'd found there that would live up to all this hype.

John fished around at his feet and handed me the crowning glory: a box of Special K cereal. Not just your run-of-the-mill

Special K cereal, oh no. This one had the face of my one and only lifelong hero, Kristi Yamaguchi, the Olympic ice-skating champion, on the front. I was elated. I turned that box into a shrine. Like a stalker, I stuffed every scrap of newspaper clipping or *Parade* magazine feature about my hero that I could find in that box and kept it in the most secure place I could think of (under my bed, obviously).

It wasn't enough to read and reread the newspaper articles and the back of the Special K box. It wasn't enough to watch the World Championship events twice a year. I didn't just *love* Kristi Yamaguchi, I wanted to *be* her. As it turned out, this required quite a bit of imagination. I owned exactly zero pairs of ice skates and had never actually seen the inside of an ice-skating rink. I was never much of an athlete, which is a kind way of saying I played right field that one year and tried out for, but never made, the cheerleading squad.

But if I wanted to pretend I was Kristi Yamaguchi, then none of that mattered. I did, as it turns out, own a pair of 1980s' Walmart-edition, pink-and-teal roller skates. With the neighborhood kids I discovered that if we scrunched all the brooms and old pairs of shoes to one side of the garage, then guess what? The smooth part in the middle was an ideal ice-skating rink! You just had to make sure the cats were out of the garage (learned that the hard way). We dragged out the old CD/cassette player and put in the Whitney Houston *Greatest Hits* CD. I had an absolutely breathtaking routine to "I Will Always Love You." I had also snuck into Mom's closet and swiped a pair of nude pantyhose, which, paired with a one-piece bathing suit, made me look as darn near Kristi Yamaguchi as someone could in this life.

I am sure there were times Mom had to retrieve a mop from the garage and happened upon this hilarious re-creation of the 1992 Olympic ice-skating event. The odd thing is, I never remember her laughing at us. I think Remaining Unamused at Ridiculous Displays is one of those parental skills you get really good at over time. At first glance, this little scene of eleven-year-old Kristi Yamaguchi–wannabes seems like nothing. *I am here to tell you it's not nothing.* What we were doing when we were squeezing ourselves into pantyhose and using Dad's hair gel to make sleek ice-skater buns mattered.

We were dreaming.

That is different but along the same lines with what I saw the other day when I was folding the linen napkins. My daughter proudly walked in with a little getup she had put together. She had taken the cushioned crib bumper that went on her baby doll's crib and wrapped it rather impressively around her entire body so that it made this dual-purpose queen's robe and a baby carrier. In the front of her was her stuffed Piglet, perched as comfortably as a forward-facing six-month-old at the grocery store. On top of her head was a plastic tiara, which perfectly completed her outfit as "Piglet's mom, who is also queen of the world." She was beaming.

Both of these are the same, Kristi Yamaguchi and Piglet's queen-of-the-world mom. And mom and me. Her coming out to mop, and me folding the towels, both of us thinking *these* tasks were the important ones of the day. But what if the wrapping of the crib bumper and the squeezing into pantyhose—what if they were the most-mattering things?

I think they are, and here is why.

First, *moments like that build creativity.* I am not a corporate boss of anything, but if I was, I would want employees who could devise a creative ending to a problem. This isn't an inborn trait like brown eyes. It can be honed, and that's precisely what is being done in garages with wannabe figure skaters. They are expanding mental, creative, and imaginative muscles.

Second, *moments like these help kids escape in a healthy way.* Childhood is wonderful but fraught with real and imagined losses. Things like parental strife, classroom bullies, anxieties about the next stage, loneliness, and heartbreak over a friend who moved. Using your imagination helps you escape the real life in front of you, carrying you to a different one, just for a bit. No, we can't and shouldn't live there, but just for a bit, our minds are transported to a different place, a safer one.

And finally, *moments like these help kids dream.* It is stretching the muscles to say, "You aren't this yet, but you could be." Isn't this the best gift an imagination can give someone? Here's how you can help.

- Give them permission to imagine. Talk about it with them openly and often.
- Open up time and space to create and dream. Don't be running around forever and ever. They need opportunities to simply hang out with no agenda.
- Dream with them. You don't have to tell unathletic ten-year-olds that they can be Olympic medalists. But underlying every conversation should be the idea that "Yes! God made you to do something great! I wonder what you'll do?"
- Be their biggest cheerleader. Most importantly, don't ever, ever laugh when you go looking for your mop and you find your daughter wearing your pantyhose because she's in the Olympics. (At least not until you shut the door.)

Dreaming about what you want to be when you grow up is pretty much hardwired into kids—it seems to come with the package. But it can become a truly beautiful gift we give our children when we participate. Not just dreaming with them but also fanning the flame of imagination and giving them space to enjoy a creative childhood. Relishing reading. Protecting play. Taking charge of technology and using it well. Let's jump into ways we can do that for our families.

Their Work Should Be Play

Kids do not play like they used to, and it's a shame. Emerging research continues to suggest that play is being forced out of childhood in lieu of more academic learning or general busyness. This busyness comes in the form of skill-based classes, clubs, and camps—and kids are not the better for it.[1]

It's not that grown-ups are being mean and cruel, yanking kids off swing sets and out of cul-de-sac kickball games just to be spiteful. That is not it at all. Play is getting the boot because people think it's better for kids if they do more "important" things instead. The irony is, kids learn most effectively through play.

It's easy to talk about people in general and to pretend it's the general public making the mistakes. It's harder to realize you do it too.

When people meet my five-year-old daughter, the first question they ask is "Are you in kindergarten?" The answer is no. And I don't feel badly about that decision, but I do feel an underlying need to be super productive with this prekindergarten year. We need to get ready. Since I am both her mom and her teacher, I have a unique insight into the pressures that this brings. There is no one else who will get her ready. You can't call it a day with letter-learning and hope someone else does the hard work of it tomorrow because that someone else is you, and it won't feel any more exciting tomorrow morning than it does now. I am hearing stories of friends' kids entering kindergarten "behind," struggling to stay on pace with their peers. My daughter's classmates are imaginary, but one day they will be real, and my competitive nature doesn't want her "behind" anyone.

And so some mornings we are at the big brown table with a very academic-looking workbook, trying to figure out the patterns with the baby seals and the mommy seals. I did a naughty thing. I knew she was tired, but I felt stressed that she surely should be able to do the mommy-seal, baby-seal pattern by now. And I pushed her. Her little shoulders drooped down, her eyes got teary, she put her hand dramatically to her forehead (we aren't emotional at all in our family), and she cried, "I can't do it! I don't understand it!" I have read enough education materials to know that we had reached the end of productive learning and the best thing we could do would be to stop. But I didn't. (I told you, so naughty!) I was able to procure a few more pattern questions out of her but not without a large pool of tears and discouragement on both of our parts.

Once done, she jumped down off the chair, skipped to her toys, and began happily lining up little plastic bears in a row, jabbering cheerily to herself as she played. And it wasn't lost on me. I had pushed her too hard. I mean, sure, she will be just fine, and she does, after all, need to learn those patterns sometime. But was I really achieving the best thing?

My mother-in-law is an expert on this subject. She was a kindergarten teacher for twenty-five years. Can you imagine the number of zippers she has zipped, shoes she has tied, juice boxes she has prodded with straws, little chubby hands she has helped to form letters? Her patience astounds me. This is what my mother-in-law has to say about play:

> Play is what kindergarten is for! They shouldn't be sitting down and doing worksheets. They need to be running and painting and mixing and asking questions and then when they're all worn out, taking naps! Play isn't a distraction from their work. It *is* their work, and it prepares them in so many ways for skills they need later on in life.[2]

I find it fascinating to observe the contrast between past decades of kindergarten and what it aims to be today. My friend Jessica is a kindergarten teacher in a wonderful charter school that emphasizes the old-fashioned good stuff: a slower, more natural pace of learning; sensory play; imagination; fine and large motor skills; and social skills. These are wonderful things, but it means fewer worksheets, less homework, and a slower path to reading. How do parents feel about this? Jessica says that quite often they hate it. It worries them that their kids may be falling behind. It makes them nervous that their kids don't have homework. Jessica tells them, "When they get home, let them bake or swing on the swings and play in the neighborhood. They don't need any more school."[3]

What I find interesting is that not only do these children all eventually learn to read but their school is one of the most successful and sought after in the area.

There's no doubt about it, play pays off.

And may I add one more thing to consider regarding the preschool question? The last few years have shown a push for early preschool attendance. So much so that these words may actually sound like heresy. But I will say them anyway: if you do not want to send your kid to preschool and prefer to keep him or her at home with a day rich in conversation and play—going to parks, making cookies, visiting the library, reading books, taking naps, mashing Play-Doh—I do not believe you are doing your child a disservice. On the contrary, your child is doing just precisely what a little three- or four-year-old should be doing: *playing.*

How to Raise Readers

The other day I had to go into Verizon Wireless to get a new phone. I would like to talk about how my new phone cost as much as a used yet extremely drivable car, but I won't because that is not the point of this discussion. Nor is the fact that my phone suddenly started having "not enough storage" to do anything, which I strongly suspect was because the virtual gerbils realized I had owned it for four years and they needed to trigger me to get a new one. These things are really annoying, but, again, they are not the point of this chapter.

What I do want to share with you is this. I had to take my kids in with me on this errand. I knew it was going to take a while, so I strategically brought two things in with me: a stack of books and a handful of lollipops. When I pulled in to the parking lot, I said, "Kids, you're going to read these books, and you're going to behave. And when we get done, you get to have these lollipops. Got it?" They got it.

I was at the part where the Verizon people were magically transferring my old pictures to my new phone when the girl helping me looked over my shoulder. Her face was overcome with shock. "Are your kids all reading books right now?" I do not think her eyes could have gotten any wider. "Are you like a magical parent? This is unbelievable. Hey [person working at the next register], look at those kids reading! Can you believe this?"

I definitely enjoyed a few minutes of feeling like I was a unicorn parent with angel children. Then one of the angel children got bored with her elephant book and started pulling the leg hairs of another child, who was trying to read his Magic Treehouse book. Child 2 hit Child 1 over the head with the (fortunately paperback) book, and I was back in reality like one of Cinderella's horse-rats at midnight. I had lost my perfect parent award for sure, but the store employees were still overcome with disbelief that three kids could sit without devices and read for twenty minutes. One said, "I literally don't think I have ever seen kids come in here and not be on a device."

This is not the kind of story I like to tell. I am the furthest thing from a unicorn parent with angel children. (That would be my sister Jenny.) I prefer sharing my own foibles with you all because I have some sort of fear that you'll lay down one of my books and roll your eyes and not feel that you could ever (or would ever) want to do anything you are reading.

But this story is important. It is more important than me not wanting to be that author who tells an annoying look-at-me story. Honestly, if I think about it enough, I get teary-eyed. *Reading is a dying art.* The fact that a group of store employees cannot remember the time they've seen kids reading books during their free time— this should be absolutely heart-wrenching.

And why, exactly? What does reading do? There are studies and statistics galore on the importance and the positive impact of reading on children, how it affects brain development, increases empathy, and more, but I'm looking at this less as a professional and more as a mother.[4]

Why does reading matter? What does it add to childhood? I have a few thoughts.

- **Gratitude**

  This year my kids and I read *Small Steps: The Year That I Got Polio*. They were hooked on this book from paragraph one. They'd stomp their feet and yell and plead that I read "one more chapter!" (This is not a normal occurrence.) We were astonished, and sobered, to read that polio-infected kids in the 1960s spent years lying down in a machine called an iron lung if they were not able to breathe on their own. We thought about all we would miss seeing and doing and hearing if we were stuck in an iron lung for the rest of our lives. Suddenly piano lessons and bed-making and other dreaded chores seemed not quite so bad.

A friend of mine recently shared that she was concerned because her kids struggled with being contented. They live in a very affluent area, and, compared to their friends, they felt like they didn't quite get to do or buy enough. My suggestion to her was to read to them, to show them stories of kids who really struggled and suffered. Reading is like making friends with people who are vastly different from you. Your own empathy and gratitude are widened immensely.

• **Self-discipline**

You can't fast-forward reading. It's not an instant-reward system. A really good book requires work and persistence. It asks something of you and grows a skill in you.

• **Hope**

Stories give us hope because they remind us that things can be different. They help us get outside of ourselves, believe in change and growth, and recognize that the world we see in front of us is not all there is. When I was eleven years old, I was really lonely for the first time. We'd moved five hundred miles and five states away from my childhood home and all my cousins. I had all of four boys and one antisocial girl in my small sixth-grade class, none of whom returned my awkward smiles. By the grace of God and the public library, I did find one kindred spirit friend in sixth grade: Anne Shirley. There are eight books in the Anne of Green Gables series, and I know this because I read every one, sitting with legs crossed on my bed after school in the lonely winter of sixth grade. These books were more than company; they were healing.

Does it matter what kind of books your kids read? Are they all created equal?

In the homeschooling world there is a somewhat heated discussion regarding the balance of reading material. How many good books versus unproductive, "uneducational" reading should a parent allow? Many parents are vehemently against much of today's youth literature, graphic novels, and kiddie books. I have a different take on this. I think it's okay to enjoy both, as long as the content isn't inappropriate. (Which it often is! You have to check.) I have found the "uneducational" reading is often a road to the good stuff. A life of reading only Star Wars graphic novels, Cam Jansen, and the Babysitter's Club would really be sad. But I have let my kids, especially in the early stages of reading, find on-level books that are easy and fun to read. Then I make them read fifteen minutes of a book that I like, and they end up getting hooked.

Let me share some practical tips that I believe will encourage your children to read and read widely.

- **Set the example.**

  I've always been an avid reader . . . until I had kids. There were several years in there that I stopped reading. I mean, I read WebMD articles about how long strep is contagious, and recipes for meat loaf, and magazines that were in the bathroom. But books? Ha! I barely had enough time to shave my legs. That's just how it was for a while. And then I started teaching my oldest to read. And I would say, "Books are awesome! You should read!" And I was never reading. It felt hypocritical, so I started reading again. Sometimes I feel guilty reading, which is really odd, but I do. I guess it feels like I should never read if there are dishes in the kitchen sink (which there always are) or clothes in the dryer (same). I have slowly realized that I am a walking example of how to do life as a grown-up, which is terrifying. I want them to be grown-ups who read books at night and not scroll their phones endlessly.

- **Be the parent.**

    Sometimes you have to make kids do things that they don't like at first. I can't tell you how many times I've made my kids start reading a book that they didn't want to read, and then they'll disappear for a few hours, and I find them sucked into the book they didn't like. To get kids to read, sometimes you have to make them. This is that whole thing about how you are the parent, so don't be afraid. So far my rule has been that if you still don't love it after four chapters, then you don't have to read it. Eventually in school they'll have to keep at it, but nine times out of ten the classics I make them read, they eventually do come to enjoy.

- **Provide good choices.**

    I have often said that whatever my failures as a mother (and there are so, so many), at the very least I am consoled by the fact that I have brought them to the library every month. We return the stack of forty or so books and then check out just as many new ones. The library truly is magic. It's not free, though, not for our family. We leave a book outside in the backyard about every four months, and there is a Hank the Cowdog CD that I promise you some monster snuck into our house and ate *because it is not here.*

- **Don't be afraid to give incentives.**

    Last summer everyone in the family who read ten books got to buy a brand-new book. Parents included! Sometimes you just have to read because you have to read, but I also think it's great to offer incentives, especially during a season (like summer) where free time abounds.

- **Limit the options.**

Which brings me to my next point. If you want them to read, then minimize, or sometimes hide, the other more fun options. In our home you have to earn your TV time. It is a long and complicated system, so much so that it would take pages to explain and my editor would make me delete it. But the bottom line is we have chosen certain tasks that our kids must do to earn time watching TV or playing the video games on the camera that my mom gave my son—the one that we didn't know had video games (ask me how I feel about the camera with secret video games). Anyway, the TV is not perpetually accessible, nor are apps or video games. If they were, books would be far less interesting. I am not sorry about this apparent trickery. It has made all of us read way more. This is a gift I never regret.

When I think about what I'd most want you to take away from this little essay on reading, one thing sticks out to me. It's that part in the middle about being a good role model. Here's an analogy. I really want my kids to eat vegetables with every meal. I want them to do that now, to be healthy, and I want them to grow up to be grown-ups who eat vegetables with every meal. But here's the thing. Sometimes I don't want to eat a side salad of spinach with my bean burrito. I just want the plain burrito. Too much of this salad-less burrito for lunch, and the kids will start to notice. They may not say anything, and they may keep eating the carrot sticks or celery I religiously put on their plates, but I guarantee you, down the road it will start to dawn on them. "Wait a minute. Mom gets to make her own choices, and all she eats are burritos. With no veggies! I can't wait until I can do that when I grow up."

We can monitor and *control* things all we want, but our examples speak volumes. Eat those veggies, Mom. And read those books. They both make you feel better anyways.

The Part About Technology

A few years ago I had an epiphany at the neighborhood pool that I wrote about on my blog and on Huffington Post.[5] I titled it "The iPhone Is Ruining Your Summer" because I had just witnessed perfectly styled teenage girls completely absorbed in their iPhones—taking selfies and then settling back in their chairs to separately stare into the screens. I remembered my own days of middle school and all the fun I had, cannonballing in the pool wearing clearance-rack bathing suits and then sunbathing with my best friend, talking about nothing and everything. Please don't get me wrong; I wasn't judging the teenagers at the pool. Because if I were in their shoes, it's not likely I would have done anything a speck different. Heck, I'm a mom now, twenty years the wiser, and if I were to visit the pool with a friend and a free hour, I'd do the same stinkin' thing—be absorbed in my own device (or exert a hefty amount of willpower not to be). But it's just a shame. The first time someone could check his e-mail while waiting for a pound of ham to be sliced, *it all changed*. We may have gained the ability to order high heels at a stoplight, but we lost something too. Something meaningful. We lost boredom, and conversation, and the ability to just enjoy simple moments without documenting them.

Many of you reading this book have a luxury that's becoming increasingly rare. You remember, like I do, a childhood *without* pervasive technology. What kinds of activities did you enjoy most? What are your favorite memories? I wish I could be sitting across the table while we talked about this because I bet that before long I'd be smiling, nodding, and nearing tears. I have found there to be common threads in this kind of reminiscing.

- We played very active games with other kids. Sometimes it was cousins, sometimes neighbors, and sometimes fun grown-ups would join in. We'd play things like capture the flag, hide-and-go-seek, baseball, and touch football.

- Often we'd be doing something dangerous or dangerous-feeling outdoors.

- There was quality, uninterrupted time with parents and family—such as parents telling crazy stories, riding together in the car, a shared hobby like repairing a car, baking, or playing sports.

- Nature was often involved, with opportunities to play all day on the beach, catch fireflies (it is uncanny how many people mention catching fireflies!), climb trees, and build forts.

Noticeably absent from the list of most treasured memories are video games and afternoons of TV. (Although a good movie night shows up here and there.)

Do today's kids have these kinds of memories? According to a 2015 Common Sense Media study, American teenagers are spending nearly two-thirds of their waking hours on screens.[6] This is an incredible statistic.

This essay on technology is crucial but also tricky. I don't want to be wistfully nostalgic with no real application. *No, we cannot re-create the past.* That would be a fruitless, impossible goal. I'm not wistfully mourning the good old days with no actionable, relevant step for all of us who actually live in an age with Pandora, *Madden NFL*, and Instagram. No, the question I am asking is this: *In the new and modern world, how do we give our own kids the best kind of childhood?* I have thought about this a tremendous amount, and I have some guiding principles I'd like to share with you that begin with understanding what technology misuse does to children.

The point here is that you will need armor and ammunition and all of the military metaphors there possibly are to survive the barrage of requests for various forms of technology that you have decided against. You need to know your stuff. There have been books written on this topic, but fortunately for you, I have read a lot of them; here are the key takeaways. These are the facts you can tell your kids, your husband, your friends, and yourself in weak moments where you want to give up and do what everyone else is doing. I am indebted to Melanie Hempe, the author of *Screen Strong Solutions*, for her insights on this subject.

1. It is biologically proven that children's brains need a whole host of things in order to develop in a healthy way, and exactly *none* of these must be technology based. In order to thrive, children need touch, nature, music, empathy, friendship, language, exercise, fine motor skills, sleep, reading, family attachment, and daydreaming.[7] Quite simply, there are too many things to accomplish in childhood to spend inordinate amounts of time doing something that is not helpful in achieving the goal of healthy development.

2. More than anything, children need attachment to their parents and to other human beings. When they're tired or lonely, *Fortnite* is a sorry substitution for a good friend or a mom to talk to. If we don't build these connections, *they won't be there*. Technology on the whole does not form relationships, which are crucial to healthy development; instead, technology impedes them.

3. Ninety percent of addictions begin in childhood. What happens in childhood literally changes our children's brains.[8]

4. Contrary to how it is often explained, social media and video games are not preparation for life but rather are designed for adults. As Melanie says, "We hurt our kids when we treat them like adults. Social media was not designed for kids. It's a marketing tool. It's not a fundamental technology. You don't have to learn Snapchat to

get a job. Why are we spending so much time doing something so unnecessary?"

5. Childhood and teenage years are actually the worst time for a human to have excessive time with technology. They are still developing their identities. Their brains have not arrived at mental maturity, they struggle to make wise and measured decisions, and they are more susceptible than adults to forming permanent addictions.

6. Not all screens are created equal. Watching *Mr. Rogers' Neighborhood* is not the same as playing *Fortnite*. Practicing your typing skills is not the same as checking your "likes" on Instagram. It would be impossible for me to list all the possibilities of good, bad, and better kinds of screens because there are so many possibilities, and by the time this book is published that number will have probably doubled. Nevertheless, better screen time options have the following characteristics:

- a small and limited time slot (one episode of a show versus binging or nonstop social media access)
- a longer amount of time in between screen changes (Picture the slow tempo of *Mr. Roger's Neighborhood*, which would be good, versus the frantic, busy, loud animation of *The LEGO Movie*, which would not be as good for a developing brain.)
- coviewing events, like watching a movie or game as a family
- passive watching versus addictive, active behavior that resembles gambling—you want to keep doing the action in order to get a hit. (An example of the addictive, active media would be gaming or even achieving likes on social media. Playing a baseball video game together might

seem okay, but it is an immersive technology, where you
have to respond and engage; thus, it affects the brain
differently.) Watching a baseball game with your family
is passive and observing.

Where do we go from here? I will not leave you without practical suggestions. But first, a story.

Years ago my mom went on a diet called the cabbage soup diet.
It was pretty self-explanatory. You made a giant pot of cabbage soup,
and then you ate it for, wait for it, breakfast, lunch, and dinner.
She tried to put my dad on this diet, too, but after day two he
was so miserable we all begged her to feed him grilled cheese and
mashed potatoes. The cabbage soup diet sounded a bit radical. You
were supposed to cleanse your body for ten days with the soup and
then gradually add back desirables, such as a plain baked potato or
banana. It was a bit crazy, but, honestly, whoever thought this up
had some really good points: (1) we all eat way too much junk, (2)
we probably need a good cleanse, and (3) vegetables are good for you.

Why am I talking about cabbage soup? Sometimes you have
to suggest something radical, like the cabbage soup diet, to get
people's attention and get them healthier. Sometimes it takes an
extreme person to bring the rest of humanity to the healthier center.

I am giving you the technological equivalent of the cabbage
soup diet. I am about to say things that may sound too much,
unreasonable, extreme. But if they get your attention and make your
home a healthier place, then I don't mind being the crazy person
to suggest it. You can throw me virtual tomatoes (or cabbage—
whatever) if you don't like it. I can take it.

I want to be clear. I'm not sharing the following guidelines as the
Bible for what everyone has to do everywhere. But I do want to offer
specific boundaries. Following are what we do in our home. You'll
also find our family's Technology Manifesto in the next section.

- **Kids won't get a cell phone until they can pay for it.** Yes, I realize it takes approximately $1 million to buy a cell phone. It is so much money you would actually have to have a job to get one, which is precisely what I am saying. If they need a way to communicate with us before that point, they get a stripped down, calls-only cell phone or a watch—something with zero apps or Internet.

- **As a rule, being on a screen is not in the list of our regular activities.** It is not in our daily routine to play apps, stream video, or browse social media. There is just too much other good stuff to do. Once in a blue moon I'll let someone do this if they're sick or waiting for an appointment or whatnot. It's like birthday cake: special and rare, not everyday.

- **We will not allow our kids to play first-person shooter video games.** In general, we limit to the point of nearly avoiding video games. One time I asked my former pastor what he would do differently in parenting. (He has three grown children.) Immediately, he responded: "I would never have let video games into our home."[9] We don't own a device, so they get to use it at Grammy's house. (I have friends who only do video games on weekends, or one hour a day that you earn during the summer.)

- **Parents set the tone.** This is extremely convicting for me, but such an important piece. They are watching how we do phones. They sniff inauthenticity from a mile away. We must be able to model healthy technology use, because one day they will have phones.

I realize that things get complicated as kids get older, with all sorts of fuzzy in-between steps. (Can they browse a parent's Instagram account? How often and with what supervision? Do they play games at neighbors' houses? Are there limits on texting friends?

Do we have phones in our rooms at night?) I could give you my answers to these (Yes. Once a day while I sit next to you. No. I can read all texts. All tech stays in the living room.). But I realize the questions are constantly changing. I think the key principles remain:

1. Vastly limit technology and don't be afraid to do so.
2. Find a tribe who does what you do and encourage one another. (So important! Your kids need kids being raised like them, and you need parents raising kids like you do.)
3. Chase after a rich life outside of technology.

The bottom line is something I absolutely cannot overstate. You can chase after every other single thing in this book, but if you're failing here, your children will suffer immensely. This technology piece is the crucial piece. Tech-addicted kids don't play well, they don't attach to their families well, they are exposed to sexual images earlier, their reading suffers, their imagination is crippled. You absolutely must get this piece close to right or die trying. I don't say this to overwhelm or discourage you but because I believe it is so crucial to modern parenting. We have to be different from everyone else here.

This involves a lot of specific decisions. I am not saying if you don't do exactly as I do, then your kids are doomed. But if you are frustrated with how technology is affecting your family and have been praying for specific guidance, here is your guidance. If you want to be different in this area but you feel alone—you are not alone. You can do this. And hey, look at the bright spot; at least you don't have to eat cabbage soup tonight for dinner![10]

A Family Technology Manifesto

As your kids reach the age when they will also be using technology, I think it's a fantastic idea to come together as a family and decide, together, what you believe about the use of technology. Let me clarify a bit what I mean by "decide, together." As parents, you set the rules. It's your home, and, likely, *your* technology and wireless Internet because you pay for it! So you have the final say, and you are primarily the "steering committee" for making the decisions about how you will use and limit technology.

From there the important next step is to create a manifesto, a document that details your decisions. You might hold a family meeting to introduce your manifesto and ask age-appropriate questions, which could include things such as "How do you feel if you're talking to someone and they are looking at their phone and not at you?" "Have you ever been hurt by something someone said about you online?" "What are your favorite things to do that aren't technology related?" And then I would remind the kids that they can keep you, the parents, accountable to the manifesto as well. This document can be something you point back to and remind one another of. You could even print, frame, and display it!

Since every family is different, I won't tell you how you might construct your family's manifesto, but I will share with you the one we have designed for ourselves.

The Smartt Family Technology Manifesto

We believe in encouraging one another to use technology to help us reach our main goals in life—to love people, to love God, and to each be the best that we can be. We know that technology isn't bad or good—it's a tool that can be used well or poorly. We believe that to use it well, we need accountability. We need people in our lives to call us out in the areas where technology weakens us. We need to be able to talk openly and graciously about how we're doing and where we've failed. We need systems on our devices to help us in the areas where we are weak. We need our phones and devices to be open books—no private apps or private conversations.

Because the best parts of life happen away from a screen, we need rest from the work and play and scrolling we do on devices. We believe that intentional times and places should be free from technology so we can rest and reconnect and adventure. Our bedrooms, our meals, our holidays, and our Sundays are where we strive for mental white space.

We know that social media can be used for good or used for bad. In our family we want to use it to connect, encourage, and learn from one another. We speak kindly to someone and of someone whether they're standing in front of us or not. We use technology as a way to love other people. We treat others the way we would want to be treated. We are wise in what we post, text, or share about ourselves. Nothing will be hidden that is not revealed. God always sees.

That is our technology manifesto. I encourage you now to think and pray through what is best for you and your family.

There's Too Much to Do to Be Glued

There is too much to do in childhood to get stuck in front of a screen. There are hopscotches to draw out and jump. There are games of kickball to play and puddles to splash. There are forts to build out of blankets and stuffed animals to line up for parades. There are lizards to catch and bubbles to chase. There are lemonade tea parties to have, letters to scribble, ballgames to win, great stories to read. There are hammocks to swing in, dandelions to pluck, pretend baby dolls to dress up and burp. There are sunsets to admire, rainbows to find, lightning bugs to run off and catch. There are bike ramps to build, kites to hold on to, mud pies to pat down and then mix up again. There are worms to dig up, big bugs to discover, bike races to have on the driveway. There are clubs to create, cartwheels to try, and so many songs to learn. There are snuggles to get and hugs to give, pumpkins to pick and presents to wrap.

Oh, there's so much to learn! How to hold your breath, your pencil, and your legs just right when you're swinging. How to do puzzles and double knots and curve balls and ponytails just like Mommy's. How to ride a bike and a horse and a wave to the shore. There are picnics to go on and adventures to have and friends to make and lessons to learn. Screens aren't all bad, but there's just too much to do to get stuck there for long.

Here is quick list of things you can do to help occupy a child without the use of technology.

Ways to Pacify a Fussy Kid, Without a Screen

1. Read her a book.
2. Arrange him on a couch with a cozy blanket and a stack of books to browse or an audiobook playing.

3. Give her a snack. (Sometimes a snack eliminates a lot of whininess.)
4. Sit him on your lap and rub his back.
5. Put her in a warm bubble bath.
6. Put him in a bathtub filled with balls or stuffed animals.
7. Build a fort of blankets and put stuffed animals, pillows, and books inside.
8. Go for a drive and let her look out the window. Nothing wrong with getting Chick-fil-A lemonade on a grumpy afternoon.
9. Give him something sensory to play with in a box—sand, water, water beads, flour, dried pasta—along with spoons or cups to scoop.

We might also call this a "Mom, I'm bored" list for those days when you're stuck inside or when nothing seems to satisfy. You can also use this list to get you thinking about your own go-to list, then keep it handy for those days you need it—because if you're a mom, one thing is for sure: you're gonna need it.

CHAPTER SIX

THE GIFT OF BALANCE

Sports and Extracurriculars Are Awesome

(Except When They're Not)

When my oldest son was five, we signed him up to play soc-cer at the YMCA. It seemed like the thing you do. I have minimal recollection from this soccer season. Just a few things stand out:

- There were about as many goals scored accidentally as there were on purpose.
- Our son had a terrible attitude one time and refused to shake hands afterward. My former-navy-captain father-in-law yanked him by the earlobe to the handshaking line with as much ferocity as I have seen him display in twenty years.

- One of my nephews was *relentlessly* aggressive . . . just not regarding the actual play of soccer. That is, he perpetually had a vicious eagle eye toward the bleachers, on his little brother, whom he suspected to be eating his fruit snacks and drinking his juice boxes. He would race over to the sidelines (mid-play, mind you) and yell, "Stop eating my chewy snacks!" He was the most aggressive player out there, for sure.

Few things are more demonstrative of a parent's unrequited love than a YMCA field on a Saturday morning in mid-June. It stuns me. This is the busiest, most run-ragged and overworked segment of society, with any one of nine hundred things they could be doing instead. These are the moms who have nursed babies every three hours all night long and who haven't had a leisurely Saturday morning in a decade. And yet they come. Lugging sunscreen and thermoses of coffee and sippy cups and all the lawn chairs and blankets and sun umbrellas and enough snacks for a car ride to Mexico. They'll heartily yell phrases like "Way to be ready!" and "Nice try, buddy!" in the most extreme of conditions—from sleet, to drizzle, to sun so terrible that the sweat drips in steady streams down sticky t-shirts.

By the way, I've focused on ball sports, but I could be talking about any number of popular kids' activities. I have a friend whose girls are standouts in gymnastics and dance, and her weeks are brim-full with competitions and rehearsals. Maybe for your family it's swim, violin, singing competitions, karting, figure skating, or theatre.

And for what? What pulls parents to partake willingly in this spectacle, in the face of sundry other more appealing Saturday morning options? Of course, I can't speak to the motivation of every single parent who lugs an often-unenthusiastic Little Leaguer to the ball field in ninety-degree heat, but a few common themes draw us to committing (sometimes *over*committing) to organized activities for our kids:

1. It feels good when our kids are involved in stuff, and it feels even better when they are *good* at stuff.
2. As parents, we have fixated on a few *particular arenas* that we think mean something. We have universally agreed, for example, that *it means something* to win a swim meet or a dance competition, to be starting pitcher, play travel soccer, or excel at piano.
3. We will willingly help our kids reach these goals in spite of tremendous personal sacrifices to our finances, comfort, or schedules.

What are we trying to accomplish with kids' activities? And is it a worthy goal? I am not an expert with all the answers. I'm right here with you, mama. But considering we are poised to spend thousands of dollars and thousands of hours on our children's extra-curriculars, it's probably worth thinking through this thing for a minute. Here are two principles I have settled on:

1. Kids' Activities Guiding Principle 1:

   We don't get our self-worth from our kids' performances. Period. You will do yourself and your kids a serious favor by getting this resolved before you ever set foot on a field or set your bottom down in a recital hall. I used to have these pictures in my head of those parents who are too into their kid's performances. These parents look like one of two things. One was the pathetic former-football-star dude who talks nonstop about that one time when he was quarterback back in the '80s and played in the Dallas Cowboys stadium. The other picture in my head was the mom who never felt popular as a kid so she lugs her overly eyeshadowed, mildly interested daughter around to dance performance after dance performance. In each case, it is super obvious that these people are finding their worth in their kids' success. None of these parents, notably, look anything like me.

And then there was the flag football team of 2018.

If you look up "big fish in a little pond" in a dictionary, you will probably see a picture of my nine-year-old son as quarterback for the YMCA recreational football league of 2018. We. Owned. It. We have a video of the game where both of my boys scored multiple touchdowns (playing on the same team = mother's dream). In the final quarter my older son threw a bomb to younger son, who ran it in for an All-Smartt-Family touchdown. I actually cried in the parking lot of the YMCA. It was just about the most wonderful feeling I had ever felt as a parent. We were happy! We were successful! People were high-fiving us and admiring us and smile-nodding down the field at us. Never mind that it was one teensy little recreational flag football league. My kids were *good*! They were talented! One of them the next Tim Tebow, probably! I wanted more of that feeling.

I had an underlying hunch it maybe wasn't so healthy and a similar underlying hunch it may not be sustainable over the next decade. I consulted with a friend at church with two older boys. "How do you keep it healthy?"

His words hit me like a brick: "I actually hope that my son loses and messes up sometimes. I want him more than anything to learn character. You don't learn character from always winning."

You hope your son loses? With people watching? Are you superhuman? I was so impressed by the freedom he had. He was not tied to his son's performance as a goalie. It didn't validate his worth as a human. Maybe his son would do well! Maybe he wouldn't! No skin off his nose! That kind of detachment was curiously appealing.

And it struck me, too, that this kind of freedom is a tremendous blessing to our kids. Do I show more excitement when they win than when they lose, even if they tried their very best? Do I show them that success is the ultimate goal? We have to get our hearts right. Our kids see right through our words, to our disappointment or our unconditional approval. Believe me, I understand that this is counterintuitive and may take a lot of effort. If you find yourself getting overly emotionally invested in the outcome of a game or event, or worse, in your child's performance in some game or event, take deep breaths and 1000 mg of a chill pill. And when I say take deep breaths, I mean literally walk away and take some deep breaths. Calm yourself the heck down. You are the parent. *You* are the steady assurance that things are okay. You are the reminder that there are more important things than wins and success and that life will go on after today. You be the adult.

2. Kids' Activities Guiding Principle 2:

After you get over your kids' wins being your wins, take it a step further. Keep your eyes ever focused on this fact: the most important thing is not success; it is character. Don't gloss over that last sentence because it's cliche and boring. Go back and read it again. Do you really believe that? If that really and truly is how you feel, are you living that way? Are we choosing activities based on ease for us? Or are we asking things like the following:

• What hobby or sport is going to grow the character traits that my child is needing most?

- When my kid has a good day on the field or on stage, what words should I say to him?
- When my kid has a bad day on the field or on stage, what words should I say to him?

I have one son who is very hard on himself. He feels losses and mistakes more deeply than my other two. I wanted to encourage him in the right things. I was pondering this one Saturday and had a real "mom win" moment in the flower aisle at Trader Joe's. This grocery store has a wonderful line of funny and encouraging greeting cards. I picked up a few of these cards, and after his games I would stick one on his pillow. Each time, I wrote the same thing at the end. "I love you whether you win or lose." Sometimes we overthink parenting, but never disregard the power of a silly card with watercolor owls on it and a simple affirmation. (I still, by the way, have the one my mom gave me during my college applications days. It has a picture of sheep wearing knee pads and says, "I'm on my knees praying for you.") So find creative ways to remind everyone of the most important things.

I have a friend with a ten-year-old daughter who sings like Whitney Houston. I asked my friend if she's tempted to send her here and there and everywhere in a quest to make it big. She said, "I would have done that a long time ago if I wanted to. I don't want that life for her. We'll go slowly at our own pace and see what God does."[1]

What trust! What patience! Character first; don't get distracted by wins. It's a sure way to be a blessing to your spouse, your kid, your coach, and the other parents. Here are specific ways to value character over success:

- **When the event is over, talk about their character and behavior way more than their performance.** Not just in vague generalities, like "you played well" (which is the kid equivalent of husbands telling wives, "Honey, you look beautiful every day."), but in specifics: "How did you feel when you fell down in the performance? I loved how you got right back up." "I liked how you cheered for James since he hasn't scored all season."

- **Cheer well for the other participants when they do well, including the other team.** I'm still learning this one and am so impressed when a parent on the opposing team cheers, "Great hit!" for one of us. It's like seeing a double rainbow or something. You feel all warm and magical inside.

- **Enthusiastically compliment other parents.** This is a clear and powerful way to minister to and encourage your own peers, folks. I could write down verbatim the compliments other parents have given my children throughout the years. It is that powerful!

How Much Is Enough?

The first time I attended a baseball tournament, I was stunned. It is a whole thing. Now, granted, you're there for like seven hours, sometimes over multiple days, so you do need to be prepared. But the coolers and tents and lawn chairs and battery-powered fans and Bluetooth speakers and life-sized cutouts of the nine-year-old players and all the grandmas and grandpas and puppies and slushie machines and hot dog rotisseries . . . oh my goodness! These people are committed. And I know there are equivalents of this scene in the worlds of dance, swim, volleyball, cheer, gymnastics, theatre, and more. If you want an all-consuming hobby for your kid (and your family), you can find one in a jiffy.

This brings up questions. How committed do you get? How far do you drive? How much do you pay? Do you miss the reunion, the church service, the vacation, the birthday, the wedding? Will your kids burn out? What does it take to be a success, and is it worth it?

I do not know the answers to all of these questions. I am not writing these words as a mother of grown children, having already navigated these sticky issues with kids who did, or did not, secure volleyball scholarships. As I sit in Panera on this Saturday, I am writing with the angst of a parent currently debating whether or not to sign up my eight-year-old for a summer Challenge baseball league that plays on Sundays, a day we choose to reserve for worship and family time. I capitalized the "Challenge" part so you would notice that it's the league for super-gifted baseball players. My son had to make the team, and he did make the team. Never mind that I have the athletic ability of a snail and that my husband's genes are 100 percent in play here. You can bet that when my son throws the first pitch in a rec league game, I am yelling with extra volume so everyone around knows that the pitcher—he is *my* son, thank you very much.

You see, I didn't quite get a good taste of it in the early years of competitive activities—*how fun it is to have a talented kid*. I didn't quite get that in the beginning, but I do now. It's nearly intoxicating, actually. It is the reason this mom who said we would never miss church for silly things like sports found herself seriously reconsidering it. A Challenge team? For really good players only? Now, let me think about that.

As we think about what to commit to, we have a few things that guide our thoughts.

- **Choose your activities wisely.**

  When I recently felt apprehension about our family's imminent headfirst dive into the Wide World of Sports, I did what any self-respecting modern mother would; I asked for advice on Facebook. One of my friends has five sons, all wanting to do different things. Knowing that it could drive parents to their actual graves if they committed to doing everything their kids felt an inkling to do, she set a boundary. In addition to the common "one activity per season per kid" rule, she offered deeper wisdom: "Decide what you are trying to instill in your child through the activity." Read that over again. Common sense, but such wise advice.

  For example, when I think about my own kids, baseball is a wonderful way for both of my boys to learn life lessons right now. They're different lessons, though, for each child. One son needs to learn to shut his trap when it's not his turn to talk. He also needs to learn structure and time management and getting all his assorted things to the right place on time. The other son needs a confidence boost. He needs an activity in which he is not overshadowed by other siblings or cousins and in which he can achieve improvement. For these boys, baseball fits what we are working on individually with each of them. I love this paradigm shift because it also allows me to be focused on the right thing. Maybe you lose a bunch of games. So what? You're not working on winning; you're working on obeying the coach! Success!

In this vein, I think it's wise to always keep one eye on your family mission statement (see an example of one in the Resources) and make choices based on that. Activities serve us and our goals, not vice versa. When an opportunity comes up, does it serve what we are trying to accomplish as a family? If no, get the heck out, no matter how compelling it is. Do we just always do swim team because it's what we do? Swim team isn't the boss of us. We don't have to do stuff because we've always done it. What are you wanting to accomplish during this season for your family? What serves that goal?

My friend Hudson is a gifted athlete. I was shocked to hear him say, "Yeah, sometimes I wish I hadn't played so much baseball in my life. There was all this pressure to 'play baseball in college' and then I did that and there was nothing after that to dream of. I almost wish someone would have set the goal bigger."

I have to be honest with you. This conversation was a turning point for me. Here is a person who achieved everything on paper that many of us wish for our kids. He won the awards and the competitions and made the cuts and (dream of dreams) played on a good college team. And he says, "Then what? It was over." He even went so far as to say, "Athletics are great, and they do teach important things, but I want bigger dreams for my kids."[2]

Those of us raising talented kids should pay attention. I don't believe my friend is an anomaly, either. I've asked several successful athletes, and I get similar reactions: "It was fun, but it was a lot of baseball/football/gymnastics/dance, and I'm not sure it was really worth it." I am certainly not saying that activities are not worthwhile. Of course they are! They teach many fundamental skills and keep kids busy in a mostly good way. But what if being a recreational athlete who plays here and there and has a good time is more than enough of a goal?

- **Release the control.**

To be honest with you, I get nervous saying no to opportunities for my kids. What if they get behind? I want them to be successful. Here is where I have landed with that. It has to do with my faith, so if you do not share that perspective this may sound a little irrational. I have begun to accept that we must have faith that God is guiding our kids' futures and release the control to him. We must not think that if we don't get our kids in the right sport/team/league/teacher/class/competition, then we're at risk of messing up their futures, especially if we have prayerfully come to a conclusion. Sometimes this means that we say no to opportunities that seem wonderful, and we trust that God will make up the slack. Sometimes it means saying yes to ones that feel a little different from what we had planned.

This year in our homeschool we read the book *Christian Heroes Then and Now: Eric Liddell*, by Janet and Geoff Benge. In case his name isn't familiar, Eric Liddell is the man behind the movie *Chariots of Fire*. You may or may not be aware of the story. Eric refused to compete in his primary running event in the Olympics because it was scheduled to occur on a Sunday. This kind of religious devotion is mind-boggling today, even to Christians. He staunchly, quietly believed that it would not honor God to race on a Sunday. Guess what happened? He instead competed in a different event and won the gold medal. (Side note: he was a remarkable man, and I recommend reading this book.)

I cannot promise that if we do the right thing with our kids they'll go on to surprise everyone and win gold medals. I can kind of guarantee that will probably *not* happen. But the deeper principle remains. Can God accomplish what he wants with our kids if we don't do everything on paper that we "should"? Yes, he can. And I believe he will.

And if I can take it a step further, isn't this the essence of parenting? Don't we do our best to make wise choices, and then we lay our kids down before God begging him to show up and work in their lives? I want to be courageous enough to make risky, illogical choices about my kids' futures when they're called for. I don't want to be oppressed by the tyrannical you-have-to-do-this-or-else feeling that invades me so easily.

- **Think long and hard about missing church.**

If you have kids and your family has chosen to attend church, then you will likely face decisions at some point as to when it's okay to be a church-skipper. I am just one little mom not very far along in this journey, so I will certainly not offer concrete conclusions about missing church. I believe that is for each family to navigate individually.

But here is what I know for sure. I miss my friends when they're not at church. I noticed the family who started playing travel soccer and was gone for seasons at a time. I missed them. We all did. Your decisions and mine to miss church don't just affect our individual families. Your empty pew— people see it. And not just others in your local church. Your kids are noticing too. Your kids see what matters to you, how you make decisions, what is worth it and what is not. It is something weighty to keep in mind. We are teaching them what is important.

Goodness, all of this is a lot to navigate! But I want to say that no matter who you are and where you are, there is someone to help you in these types of decisions. I am always so overcome at the tender, condescending love of God. We often use the word *condescending* in a negative way, but what I mean here is that God doesn't need to, or have to, bother with our little decisions about varsity tennis or that competitive swim team. He shouldn't have to care. Yet he does. We have his assurance: "If any of you lacks wisdom, you should ask God, who gives generously to all without finding fault, and it will be given to you" (James 1:5).

Let us ask him and trust that he will guide us. Let us release our kids' performances and successes from our control. Let's not look to them to validate our worth. Let's prioritize the health of our families over the idols of success and activity. Let's continue to remind our kids that there are things more important than being the best and cheer them on for things that matter, like character and kindness. Even if they lose every single game in the season.

The Benefit of Failure

I didn't think I cared if my kids failed at sports. I mean, come on, I am better than that. I am literally writing the book on it. Well, this year my oldest son played on a flag football team. It was a league for fifth and sixth graders, but I think some of the other teams forgot that their sons were actually in high school and accidentally signed them up to play against my son, who looked like a miniature elf out there on the field.

The first game we got annihilated. "Oh well," we said. "That must be the best team in the league." The next week we were annihilated again, twice, in a doubleheader. It started to look and feel embarrassing. We were getting picked off left and right. It seemed like our flags were dropping at the slightest tug, but everyone else's was glued on. Was this some sort of practical joke? "Hey, everyone who plays the Chiefs gets permanent flags that can't be removed, but theirs can. Hahaha!" It felt like that was what had happened.

The parents on my son's team were friends of ours—all upstanding, mature grown-ups who cared more about building character than their children's success on recreational flag football teams. *Hypothetically*, that is. Realistically, it just felt awful. There is nothing wrong with a loss here or there, the kind where you say afterward, "Well, we played hard, but at the end they just edged ahead." This was more like, "All of our kids are just awful at football, but we didn't realize it until this exact moment in time."

We lost one game seventy-one to seven. At least that was my last count. Interestingly, this was the week I had planned to write this exact essay—on letting your kids fail. It is hard to see your kids fail. It is hard because we love them dearly, and we know that success feels more wonderful than getting your tail kicked. It is hard because a teensy part of us enjoys having kids that are good at stuff. It is hard because no one fails in a vacuum, and people see things and think things. (Or we imagine that they see things and think things.)

My premise here is that we have it backward. Failure is a gift. Being bad at things is a gift. Not winning is a gift *even more than winning is a gift*. If this is true, which I believe it is, it means that *this* football season, where we have suffered five humiliating losses and no wins, is better for all of us than one in which we are winning games left and right. It means maybe I should post the pictures on Facebook and boast, "Great news! Five games in a row where we've been pummeled!"

Okay, I won't really do that. But I should be grateful for the losses, and here is why: Failure builds character. Failure encourages hard work. And failure is a normal part of life.

Little children are not born little prodigies, miniature super-stars, or advanced masters. They have work to do. They mess up. They spill things, they run and trip, they scribble and scratch it out, they swing and miss. And this happens because they are learning! Learning, growing, falling down and getting up—this is all part of the dance of childhood. Children should not be placed upon stages and expected to perform perfectly.

And yet I often see that kids, and their parents, have lost a tolerance for failing. As a result, you have kids who don't know how to work through a loss, who are devastated by failure, who feel pressured to do things perfectly, and who lack the grit to try again. In his book *The Collapse of Parenting*, Leonard Sax states, "Fragility has become a characteristic of American children and teenagers to an extent unknown 25 years ago."[3]

My friend Karen manages a Ben & Jerry's ice cream shop and employs a large number of high school and college students. Karen says her main challenge in working with young adults today is that they cannot deal with failure. They haven't had experience fail-ing at small things in life, and therefore they cannot deal with the possibility of failing on a larger scale. They've grown up with consolation trophies, bumper bowling, and unscored sports games, where failing is taken out of the equation, so they basically believe the world will end if they do fail. As a result, Karen notes, "They lie, hide their mishaps, or worse, don't even try. As an employer, I'd much prefer the ones, honestly, who aren't afraid to take initiative or take a risk, even if it means they may mess up."[4]

Parents need not be so terrified to let their kids fail. As a middle school teacher, I witnessed examples that were comical: Student sleeps through the whole book of *Treasure Island*. Me: "Okay, your *Treasure Island* create-your-own board game is due in two weeks!" Same student turns in a laminated, life-sized game of *Treasure Island* Twister with complicated questions written in suspiciously perfect penmanship. Me: "I'm gonna take a stab in the dark. Did your mom help with this? A little?"

And why did she help? Because Mr. Hates Reading's mother has an unfulfilled longing for literature homework? I am thinking it is less that and more that she does not want to see her kid fail. She could have said, "It looks like you have a project. If you don't have the bulk of it done by such and such date, then you will lose your something-or-other privileges." But she didn't. Why? Because it was easier to make a homemade life-sized Twister board than to enforce a consequence. And I feel you, Mom. I totally agree with this equation. Give me the Twister project any day. But in the long run, we are harming more than we are helping.

In some ways that's not the best example because, from what I recall of Mr. Hates Reading, he didn't care too terribly much about my *Treasure Island* project. But what if it involves something (*gasp*) the child really, really wants? What if it means letting him be cut from a team? Missing a big game? Not going to the party because he didn't hold up his end of the bargain? Can we step aside and allow our kids to suffer consequences when it's needed?

When I was ten, my parents signed me up for the softball league that played next to the soft-serve ice cream stand. I was horribly unnatural at softball and hated it all (except for the free after-game twist cones). It was clear I would never be great or even not horrible at softball, so I stopped playing. And that was the end of that. My foibles weren't over after the softball field; I wrecked a go-kart at age thirteen and got Cs in penmanship and science all through elementary school. Notably, these failures were essentially nonevents at home. My parents weren't devastated if we were average at things.

It is a powerful gift to let someone fail sometimes. I wonder if we need more firm pat-on-the-back assurances to let our little ones try things, mess things up, drop the ball, suffer the consequences, get paint on the table, add too much flour to the brownies, be the slowest kid in the lap pool, maybe even (*gasp*) get a D on a history test every so often. Maybe us high-achieving (see also "helicopter") parents need to take a chill pill and reorient the goal: goodbye, perfection; hello, your reasonable best. And maybe one thing that means is that instead of more classes, more tutoring, more private lessons or all-star teams, maybe our kids need more opportunities to try and to fail and *the deep assurance that they are accepted just the way they are.* The irony is, this quiet partnership fosters an environment where true excellence can grow—the excellence we were hoping for in the first place.

How do you let your kids fail, exactly? You give them opportunities that stretch them. You don't freak out when they spill something, break something, lose a game, or fail a test. You allow them to own up to what happened, and you respond with grace. And then you let them try again.[5]

CHAPTER SEVEN

THE GIFT OF GRIT

Instilling Work Ethic, Handling

Failure, and Other Lessons from Our

Neighborhood Pet–Sitting Business

I have a friend who makes me have mom envy in all the right ways. Her kids are always doing stuff that I've been meaning to do with my kids. The other day she said, "Titus walks the neighbor's dog every day, and he makes forty dollars a week! He's so proud to put his money in the bank, and then we even invest some in Stockpile, a beginner low-risk stock market app." (See what I mean? Did you get a little bit of mom envy?)

I mused on this for the next week. "Hey, boys," I said. "Did you know that Titus makes forty dollars a week walking a dog? Did you know that if he wants something, he has money to buy it? How would you like that, guys?"

One son said, "Mom, that would be amazing! If I had my own money, I would go to the grocery store and get eight mangoes and eat them all by myself." The other son said, "I'd buy a mechanical bull to ride." With these particular visions dancing in their heads, it didn't take long for them to dream up their own little entrepreneurial venture. With a little (okay, a lot) of help, they designed and printed flyers we would put into mailboxes.

"Two responsible boys looking for odd jobs," it claimed. I personally added the "responsible" part in there, and I felt a teensy bit guilty about it but also a teensy bit not because I knew I would hover my own responsible self around during the jobs and make sure no pets or houseplants died on a Smartt's watch.

We all waited expectantly for our first ~~victims~~ customers. Finally two different neighbors were going out of town and needed someone to watch their pets. Easy enough. The boys daydreamed about how they would spend their earnings. They couldn't wait to get more jobs. This was so easy! So fun! Working is amazing!

And then the jobs actually started. While on vacation the two families wanted us to watch their dogs: Pepper, Pickles, and Tina. Tina did a terrifying trick where she "smiled" and it looked like she was going to viciously tear into you with her little terrier teeth.

The responsibilities were fairly simple. Water them, feed them, let them go out to pee, replace a taped-on bandage, and tie a sock around a bloody paw injury. (Okay, that part was not so simple.) I went with the boys the first few times, and then I figured they were capable of doing it alone.

Everything went fine until Pepper's dad (also known as my brother-in-law) came home. My son walked in the door minutes later, red-faced and teary-eyed, barely holding it together.

"Mom, Uncle John said when he came home, the lights all were on, and the back door was wide open. He was *not* happy."

(Insert a fifteen-minute-long, boring conversation about how the door was left open and whose fault it was.) Here is where I started to have the beginning inklings of a thought: *Maybe my kids aren't quite responsible enough for a job.* We had a little pep-talk/lecture and then apologized to Uncle John.

All of us still tender from this unfortunate oversight, we headed over to check on our remaining customers, Pickles and Tina. I told the boys that I was going to stand there and not do anything. I was just going to watch and make sure everything was done correctly, which I fully intended to do, but things got real sticky real fast.

Pickles didn't want to go outside to pee, and Pickles weighed about 120 pounds. Tina didn't want to do anything but sit on the couch and bark at the intruders (temporary pet-sitters). My tender-hearted middle child couldn't stand the thought of her missing her dinner, so he carried it over to the couch and placed it next to her, where it promptly spilled into the cracks and crevices of said couch. Many sundry attempts were made to get Tina to go out to the bathroom, and all of them were unsuccessful. I didn't think dogs could bark at maximum volume for a sustained twenty minutes, but evidently they can. We eventually gave up on moving Tina and decided to come back later.

The boys told me they were all done. Guys, you are just not going to believe this next part. You just won't. My two *responsible* boys believed they had sufficiently completed their job and were leaving with the back door of this house *wide open.*

Another house. Another door wide open. Literally less than an hour after the *same* mistake. (P.S. Does anyone nearby need pet care? We have some open slots.) About this time my husband walked over to see how things were going. We walked the boys back in the house with Pickles and barking Tina. "Hey guys, you forgot something. What did you forget?" It took a horribly, painful long time to dawn on them. When they did realize their mistake, they of course felt awful. We came home in silence. The boys moped around guiltily in the garage. Todd and I plopped down on the couch and looked at each other. "We're doing a horrible job," I said. He laughed the laugh of someone pretending to laugh but inside being concerned. (He is an Enneagram nine, and he does this a lot.)

"How in the world have we failed so horribly? Are we raising kids who are totally careless? Will they grow up and not be able to get good jobs? This is horrible!"

Maybe your kids have never left the door wide open to two consecutive pet-sitting houses, but my guess is there have been times when you are stunned and embarrassed and frustrated with the lessons that need to be taught. I am always so surprised by how much work this parenting thing is. Kids do not parent themselves. Well, maybe some do. If you have one of these kids, you're annoying and we're going to ignore you for this part.

For the rest of us, we are earning our master's degree in personnel training and quality control. With dual minors in child psychology and patience. As I think about instilling grit in kids, a few things come to mind.

This is all very worth it and one of the main reasons that we are parents. These moments are not interruptions from the important work; they *are* the important work. The moment I realized the second back door was accidentally left wide open, I did not immediately think, *Wow. What a wonderful opportunity! Responsibility is one of the main things that I want to teach my kids, and this is an ideal situation. Hooray!* No. Actually my immediate response was annoyance. I had chicken I needed to marinate for dinner, the garage was a mess, and there were dishes in the dishwasher I needed to put away. It is hard to see these opportunities for what they really are because we have so many other things on our minds. But we *chose* to have kids. We *wanted* to have a chance to form little hearts and minds to grow up ready to face the world. This is our prime calling.

More than the chicken or the garage or the dishes. Reframing these frustrations and seeing them as what they are helps me realize they are the ideal training ground to do the most valuable job we get to do, to raise children.

This means that we have to do the hard work of parenting. First, we sat the boys down and said things that sounded like what our own parents said (but I'm sure we said it all so much better than they did). The main thing we wanted to impress on the boys was that little things matter. I have a child who rushes through everything just to get to the next (more fun) thing. We talked about how little details matter. We talked about how taking care of someone's house or property is a tremendous responsibility. We talked about how this was a perfect time to learn this because what if Dad left the doors to his company's shop wide open? He could get fired! I made the boys go write a little checklist of all the things they needed to do before leaving the pet-sitting house the next time.

Late that night my son called me upstairs and said (with sweet tears), "Mom, I don't want to do the pet care company anymore. It's too hard when you mess up." Here's what I mean about how this is prime parenting territory. Instead of a lecture, I told him about my own pet-sitting company and how one time I babysat for a cat named Morris who needed a pill jammed down his throat every day. That lightened his spirits, and I told him, "Buddy, it's way better to learn these lessons now while you're babysitting pets than grow up later and not be responsible. This is the perfect time to learn."

Work ethic itself is extremely important for our kids to learn. Not because it's a means to an end, "punching our ticket" to get to the fun stuff that happens after 5:00 p.m. No, because it is *through work* that we gain joy. Ben Sasse notes, "A hallmark of virtuous adulthood is learning to find *freedom in* your work, rather than *freedom from* your work, even when work hurts."[1] Self-discipline provides the ability for them to achieve their dreams. In *Deep Work*, Cal Newport makes the point that focused work is so rare today that if you are one of the few who can perform this intense, focused work, you will be extremely successful.[2]

As you talk to your kids about work, don't underestimate the power of sharing your own stories. This makes you relatable and authentic and brings the principles to life. You should see the dumbfounded looks on my kids' faces when I tell them that their dad doesn't enjoy going to work sometimes and that if he doesn't do his work well, he will be fired. This is one I play up to my kids. I might say, "One day you'll have a job, and if you don't do your work well, then you may have to come home and tell your kids, 'I'm sorry. We have no money to buy food.'" Yes, I make it sound overly dramatic, but, gosh, isn't it true? The goal is to develop the grit to work hard even when it is not fun.

Finally, perhaps one of the best ways to get your kids to work hard is to have them work for someone else. This makes everything feel more official, and it takes the burden off of you being their boss. The sooner they can get a *real* job with someone, the better. Word to the wise: Maybe just go behind them for the first couple of times. Just in case.

Mental Grit

Not only do our kids need the grit of manual work and job responsibilities, they also need to stretch the brain to do hard things. No surprise here—this is a lot of work for them *and us*.

A few years ago my niece visited during a homeschool morning. She was about five at the time, and she sat down at the schoolroom table and colored a picture of a unicorn for thirty minutes straight. She did each little part of the rainbow a different color, tongue out, furrowed brow, peeling down the crayon wrappers when the tips got dull. When she finished, I gaped at the finished product. It was so well done!

I was flabbergasted. I had a slightly younger daughter who, when I plopped *her* down to color, did so for thirty-seven seconds and then moaned and whined and collapsed on the table like her upper extremities had reached the uttermost peaks of fatigue. It was quite a display, and honestly pretty convincing. But as I watched my little niece working so very hard on her picture, I thought of the hours she'd practiced at her work of coloring, and the thought struck me: *Maybe I am not pushing my own daughter enough. Maybe she needs to develop her work ethic.*

Fast-forward two years. It has taken a lot of work (see also: "whining," "crying," and "parental torture"). Yes, it has been painful on everyone. But now, my own daughter has the gift of concentrating on something. Oh, she will still complain every now and then (especially when she's hungry and tired). But I am helping her learn how to focus. I feel like that was a braggy sentence to say, but, then again, I *should* be proud of this. It's a bit like the Facebook post where someone stands in their four-sizes-too-large jeans and holds out the waist. And you know there's been a lot of salmon and kale salad consumed for lunch and a lot of working out at the gym, and we all feel happy for that person. This is like that, only we're not celebrating a health victory but a mental one. And that is worth something. It has taken a lot of work on my part and my daughter's part, and now when I see her sitting on her knees at the table—nose scrunched up, chubby little fingers holding the colored pencil—I know that what I am seeing is a product of our joint hard work.

Focus isn't like eyesight, where you are what you are and it won't get better. We can *grow* in our ability to focus. It is one of the greatest gifts we can give our children, to help them focus and think. But learning a mental work ethic is a grueling, painful process, and there's no two ways about it.

It's like the pile of mulch my husband had dumped on our driveway last summer. One morning my daughter came running to me and shouted, "Mom! There are guys in our driveway and they are dumping so much dirt it is almost reaching the top of our house!" Sure enough, there *were* landscaping employees in the driveway dumping mulch, and I'm not good with spatial estimates, but I'd bet my dinner they had dumped enough mulch to landscape a small subdivision. And here's the kicker: the truck drove away.

"Yeah, I figured the boys could spread all that mulch all over our yard," my husband said, and told them he'd pay fifty dollars each when the pile was gone. *Fifty dollars!* I thought. *They're making a killing!* (By the time it was all said and done, *we* were the ones making a killing, as this averaged to about five cents an hour.)

I went outside and stared at the pile that was at least seventeen feet high. I looked at my eight- and ten-year-old boys. "Boys," I said, "you're going to spread this mulch." When I tell you we chipped away at this pile of mulch for three straight weeks, I am not exaggerating. And when I say "we," I mean that I was the one *making* people mulch, which, for the record, is way more difficult than shoveling mulch. I thought this pile would never disappear. Some mornings I would swear someone had secretly dumped more mulch during the night. Oh, what a job this was!

Developing mental grit in our children is much the same kind of work. It is thankless, sweaty, gritty, feels-everlasting work. But it is an upside-down gift we give our kids, because we help them to achieve their dreams.

When I stand over my third grader as we (again) write the *d* and *b* and *p* and tell them all apart, I think about this: one day he may be in a courtroom, in a boardroom, at an architect's desk or an author's desk (I can dream). Because he has learned to write well, his road to his dreams is just that much smoother.

Maybe one of my kids wants to be an entrepreneur. He will be able to reach this goal because he has learned to do the mental work of evaluating costs, outlining needs, conveying goals in written and spoken word. I helped him to do this.

I want my kids to be able to be anything they want to be. I don't want their lack of reading and writing skills or weakness in mathematics or small motor skills or whatever—I don't want *anything* hindering their ability to do what they dream up.

Someone did this for me. You are reading these words because I learned to think. As I sit in a coffee shop typing them, I'm working hard to focus because it is challenging to transpose thoughts into words and chapters and a book with a hopefully cohesive theme. But I am doing it and in that achieving my dream. I am doing it because my parents helped me learn to think.

This is how you help your kids reach their dreams: you do the equivalent of making them spread yet another pile of mulch although they're tired and ready to give up. You keep working at it. You encourage them: "Wow, boys! Look how strong you are to push that wheelbarrow!" Or, in this case, "Look at you! You wrote that whole paper and used all those vocabulary words. I can't believe it!" You don't let them give up. You push them just a little past the point of comfort—which, it must be noted, will be a different point from child to child.

Here are some practical ways to help stretch the mental muscles in your kids:

- **Have them memorize things that seem "too hard."** Have them learn a language, remember hymns, learn poems. They don't need to understand it all, but stretch those mental muscles, set the foundation, and they can unpack the knowledge later.

- **Make them read great books they may not naturally pick up.** I would have never chosen to read *To Kill a Mockingbird*, but thanks to eighth-grade English class, I gained a new favorite book. I have a son who vehemently protested reading *The Mysterious Benedict Society* and a week later said, with a contented sigh, "That was the best book I ever read."

- **Help them learn to concentrate.** Ben Sasse says his family challenges one another to read for sixty minutes without looking at smartphones, televisions, or computers.[3] I love how he includes the grown-ups in this, because they learn from what we do as much as what we say. We should all be continuing to develop our mental grit and focus.

Kids actually enjoy this type of challenge. Don't make it too difficult or too much for your good and not theirs. The right amount of challenge, for the right reasons, makes kids shine. Push them a little bit. Let them feel the pain of mental work. Hang in there when it seems that figurative pile of mulch is going nowhere. One day you will look over the finished job and say, "Wow! This was so hard, but we did it!"

The Surprising Characteristic
That Predicts Adult Success

A 2013 study determined that there was one single childhood characteristic that is most important in predicting success in life. It wasn't wealth, intelligence, race, or socioeconomic status. Do you know what it was? Self-control. Children who possess this skill can be tracked to achieve career fulfillment and success, better physical health, and financial well-being.[4] Think about this for a second.

As a parent, I rarely think about the virtue of self-control. I've got my eyes on the biggies, like being kind, cleaning up all your junk, being respectful, and having integrity. Self-control seems like a condiment at dinner. It's like the little ramekin of ketchup that you can add to your burger—it's definitely important, but you can get along without it.

Evidently this is not so. And if you think about it, it makes sense because self-control is at the root of what makes you do (or not do) all the other important stuff.

Recently my husband and I felt at the end of our rope with some of the behaviors we were seeing in our house. One day our children might read this book, so I won't give any names or juicy details, except to say that they all are very wonderful, and they all are very naughty. I think that covers it sufficiently. The basic gist in this most recent case was that we were seeing some unkindness, unhappiness, and anger. We had tried everything we knew, but nothing seemed to be working. Counseling felt like a horribly unfun way to spend $200, but eventually I thought, *You know, maybe the counselor can give us a few tips that we can implement, and it would make a big difference*. I turned out to be right. I half expected that he would bring everyone in and psychoanalyze us and tell us what disorders we all had and maybe do a brain scan or two.

Imagine my surprise when he asked, "Do you ever do sticker charts?" I gave a suspicious side-eye that said to my husband, *Just like we thought! Waste of two hundred dollars!* The (very wise) counselor went on to explain that even though we were seeing behaviors we didn't like (unkindness and anger), *what our children really needed was self-control.* At the root, wasn't anger an issue of self-control? And so, he continued, helping our kids to develop the ability not to lash out in anger when they were frustrated would be an incredible gift to them. He went on to describe the outline for a reward system he recommended. It was a glorified toddler sticker reward chart, where the kids had periods of the day to earn, or work toward, certain rewards.

The whole thing sounded really simplistic and, honestly, a bit disappointing compared to the brain scans and diagnoses I had been expecting. I thought we were way beyond the point where a sticker chart would work. And, after all, was it really changing anything in their character if we just gave them stickers after breakfast, lunch, and dinner? Was that really doing anything? "Oh, yes!" he said. "You are showing your kids that they don't have to be controlled by their impulses, whims, and emotions. You are showing them that they can control their behaviors. A habit like this has lifelong ramifications."

I'm not going to lie. I had to use a lot of brain power to put these principles into specifics for our family. To think up all the rewards we'd been giving out regularly for no work and then to evaluate their worth in terms of "chips" (small plastic squares I had been using for math lessons that would now be adopted for the new behavior system). But the return was fantastic, and I knew immediately that Mr. Rewards System Counselor had been onto something.

When we teach our children self-control, what we are really doing is giving them one crucial tool they need *to make their dreams come true.* "Oh, you're being dramatic, Jessica," you say. Am I really, though? What's the last dream you had? Did it come true magically, without work? Unless your dream was the lottery, I am guessing it did not.

As I type these words, I am tired. My flesh wants to eat lunch and close my eyes for a bit and then go for a walk outside. My flesh wants not to type. But aren't you glad somewhere along the line I learned the gift of self-control so you have this finished chapter to read? (Thanks, Mom and Dad.)

If you're curious about that sticker reward system I developed at the counselor's suggestion, here is the nitty-gritty to make it happen. (If you're not, then proceed to the next chapter!) Let me warn you that it may feel complicated at first to set up. It took me a few weeks to envision it and a few days to iron out the kinks. But we are going on two months, and it has made our entire home run more smoothly. It was worth the effort.

Step 1: Choose one or two specific behaviors you want your children to work on, then try to ignore the other stuff for the time being. Don't try to fix everything. Make the goal attainable and measurable. Here are some sample goals: treat your sister kindly, obey parents the first time, show respect to parents, no hitting, and don't argue back to parents.

Step 2: Divide the day into three or four chunks. Ours are after breakfast, after lunch, and after dinner. Yours may be before school, after school, and after dinner. You choose what works. The idea is that they may lose chips for one period, but no worries! They can begin again to earn the next ones.

Step 3: Every child starts the day with all of his possible chips. For example, my kids have six; they can earn two chips for each of our three time periods. If they have achieved their two goals for the time period—then they get to place two chips into their bowl. (I use little plastic math squares. You could use poker chips or bingo markers or whatever.)

Step 4: Determine what chips are worth. This was the most challenging step for me. I decided how many chips would equal a TV show, a piece of candy, a movie night, a date with Dad, or five dollars. The kids get to choose their rewards, spending their chips however they want. It's okay if you set the values and then after a week have to tweak things. And yes, some of these things may have been "free" prior to this system, but my kids never complained about the change. It was as if they liked having something to work toward.

The Importance of No

It was a whole different thing raising a girl baby versus a boy baby. When our daughter was born, even her cry was different from that of my two sons before her. From day one in the hospital, her little wail sounded higher, lighter—sweeter, even? (But don't get me wrong, it was still demanding!) I don't know if it was that she was my third baby, or that I had had two miscarriages prior, or, quite frankly, that I preemptively took my postpartum meds that round, but I relished her whole babyhood much more than I did those of her brothers. I realized how much I had missed out on during that precious first year of life with the boys. And she was a dream baby, my little sunshine. She would pose for pictures like it was her job. She loved bows and never ripped them out. She would laugh and smile and coo and babble. Oh, never was a child more doted on than this one. Her brothers adored her, aunts and uncles fawned over her, random shoppers would stop and gush over her in the produce department. Being the first girl, everything she ever owned or used was brand new and of course pink. The world smiled at this sweet ray of sunshine, and she smiled back.

And then one day I had to tell her no.

The first time I can recall, we were eating dinner. I think it was Sloppy Joes. Listen to me, Sloppy Joes have gotten an entirely bad rap. The way I make them, they are delicious. But this little pumpkin was not feeling the Sloppy Joes. Her brothers obediently finished theirs along with sautéed carrots and were each eating snickerdoodles. Oh my goodness, she wanted a cookie! I wasn't about to give a baby a cookie for the main dish of her dinner, sweet little sunshine or not. And so there we were, engaged in a dinner-time showdown of epic proportions. If it hadn't been the end of a long day on a random, exhausting Thursday, it might have been funny. It was simply inconceivable to her that she could not have that cookie. She was trying to communicate with every faculty she had that she wanted the cookie. Why was I not giving it to her? She wanted it! Did I not understand? I think it was honestly the first time it began to dawn on her that she may not get what she wanted. And it was simply blowing her mind. This had never happened in the history of her short life. She kept looking at me indignantly like, *Do you not understand? I don't want this awful dinner; I want that cookie. Am I not making myself clear?*

It has been five years since the Sloppy Joe showdown, and if I'm being honest with you, we still face remnants of that indignation when she is being offered the gift of no. It is something we are still working on. There are times when I say no just for the heck of it. Not being cruel, mind you, but just to make sure our "no" muscles are not wimping out (both hers and mine). I'll give you an example.

Today we went to a Renaissance Festival for a field trip. If you haven't experienced one, it's basically a marriage of Disneyland and the medieval period. It's sensory overload of the knights-and-fairies variety, and everything costs approximately 500 percent more than it should. You could legitimately spend $300 as a family without blinking an eye, and all you would have to show for it would be some mass-produced medieval weaponry and bones from the turkey legs you ate. I try not to be a scrooge entirely, so we did a few things here and there. I let my boys try their hands at ax throwing. Which, now that I type this, seems like bad judgment. Well, sweet little sunshine could not understand why *she* also could not throw axes. She looked around desperately; what could she do? Ah, fairy stones! She wanted fairy stones. Now! (*Whine, whine, sob, sob.*) My first instinct was to stop the bleeding, so to speak, and pacify her so the very public tantrum would stop.

And then I asked myself a question: *Which does she need more at this moment: fairy stones or to experience not getting what she wants?* I took her nicely by the hand and headed in the not-fairy-stones direction. Why would I do this? Why bother to rob this child of something that could bring her joy?

Hearing no is a gift to a child. Oh, it doesn't seem like it, but it is. Here is why.

- **Hearing no helps them be a gift to the world.** Spoiled kids aren't a gift to anyone. When we raise grateful, grit-filled, non-fragile children, they grow up to be people who do hard things. Not just like mountain climbing or whatnot, but hard things that make the world better, like enduring bootcamp and fighting for freedom, like caring for parents when they're old, like staying married when it's not fun.
- **Hearing no empowers kids.** Yes, it's true. When we say no to an immediate freebie, we have an opportunity to teach kids to work for what they want, therein making them stronger, therein giving them lifelong power to achieve more. If you've had a kid who bought something with their own hard-earned money, you know exactly what I'm talking about. That is a much bigger, more precious, and more thoughtfully purchased gift. Sometimes we say no to help them work toward the eventual yes.

I know you know this. No one wants their child to be a wimpy, spoiled brat. That is no one's intention. No, this happens because well-intentioned parents get sad that their kids can't have things. What that means is that for our kids to develop grit and self-control, we all need more of that awful feeling we get when we tell our kids no. Counterintuitive as it may seem, that's the sweet spot. Three cheers for your kids being mad at you!

CHAPTER EIGHT

THE GIFT OF MANNERS AND KINDNESS

How I Taught My Kids to Look Adults in the Eye (and Other Long-Lost Courtesies)

Last summer my boys, then nine and seven, played on a local baseball team. A few of the adults were extra friendly and would always take the time to chat with the boys. This is how it would go:

Really Nice Grown-up: Hi there! Did you have a game
yesterday?
My Child: Yeah.
(looks down at some nameless thing on the ground)
Really Nice Grown-up: Oh cool! How did you do?
My Child: Okay.
(walks away)

Oh my goodness! It made me cringe. Who raised these children? Since they were generally pleasant, respectful youngsters (*generally*, I said), I expected that they would instinctively *know* to be polite to grown-ups. Not so much. It seems kids who have this skill today are basically unicorns.

To me, nothing screams all-star kid more than the quality of being able to talk politely with an adult. Yet finding a child with good manners is often a challenge. It seems they are becoming more endangered by the day. I could speculate that it is because we humans spend less time looking at faces and more at screens, but I think I've said enough about that already.

Suffice it to say that the skills of looking people in the eye, opening doors for them, responding with full sentences, asking someone how they are, smiling at people—these things are crucial for a child to learn. It teaches them two things:

1. not to be self-centered
2. manners are essentially a way to be kind to others

Kids don't innately understand basic manners. You have to teach them. Here are the top five rules of manners that you might think your kids know, but they probably don't.

1. If you are walking through a door, stop and hold the door for the people behind you.
2. Look someone in the eye when talking to them.
3. Don't say "yeah"; use "yes, please" or "no, thank you."
4. Address adults using "Mr." or "Mrs." or "Miss."
5. Take your shoes off at the door when entering a home.

You might say that your kids are being shy when they shun adult conversation or give one-word answers. I don't doubt that there are individuals who struggle with shyness, being reticent to talk to others. But I also say we've allowed this too many times instead of calling out what their behavior really is or can be: at its core, it's rudeness.

Here's how I explained it to my kids. When a person takes the time and effort to say your name, to ask you something nice, that person is giving you a gift. They have taken something of theirs (time, effort, energy) and given it to you. How should we respond when someone gives us a gift? We should say thank you!

And one way we say thank you to this nice grown-up is by doing the following:

1. Look the person in the eye.
2. Respond with "yes, ma'am/sir" or "no, ma'am/sir." (I'm Southern; this is what we do.)
3. Offer them one additional descriptive sentence.

And, yes, those are the real words I used to talk to my kids about it. All I had to do was explain it, and my sweet little children saw the light and immediately put it in action! How do you like that?!

Just kidding. That is not what happened. Here is what happened. I ~~bribed them~~ came up with a reward system.

First, let's talk about reward systems. I have heard people say that you shouldn't offer incentives to your kids, but I disagree. I am a grown adult, and I like incentives. Not too long ago I put up a chart with smiley-face stickers on the refrigerator. If I exercised five days a week for six weeks (earning my sticker for the day), I got to go out to dinner at a really special place. Or, after I do all my work for the day, I get to watch Netflix with my husband. We adults experience incentives as a natural or manufactured byproduct for our hard work, so why not our children?

Back to the reward system for manners. I talked with our kids about why being polite matters—how it is really being kind. We thought about how busy Mr. Parrish is during the day, so how nice of him to stop and talk to us. We took our eyes off of ourselves and our unease with speaking and put them onto someone who was being thoughtful.

We discussed the three steps of talking to a grown-up (noted on the previous page). Then we practiced them. We took turns being the grown-up and did this rightly and wrongly until we were plenty goofy about the whole thing. And then I introduced the incentive. At any point, if we were out in public and I heard them do the preceding three things, they'd earn a sticker. Twenty stickers equaled one's choice of either a pack of baseball cards or a small LEGO surprise pack. I'd explain what that last item is, but it will, of course, be outdated and not cool by the time this book comes out. The point is, both are small, less-than-five-dollars, end-of-the-checkout-line items that my children would normally beg for and have no hope of getting, except on some random day Nanna came to visit. This system gave us a plan.

If you don't like my prizes, then think of your own. It doesn't have to be a monetary reward, either. Maybe you do a big production at dinner and honor a kid with a red plate and a Polite Family Member of the Day speech. As lame as that sounds, I bet you they beam and smile through the whole thing. Whatever you do, devise some way to reward your little ones for preserving the dying species of manners.

The Power of Our Words

Shortly after I had my first child, I went to Mom's house for a visit. My son, who was about a month old, had been so fussy that day. I was shushing/rocking/swaying him, trying in vain to get him to sleep, and I just couldn't take it anymore. "Mom!" I said loudly. "He is just such a fussy baby. What is wrong with him? He is so grumpy, and so fussy, and just awful today."

She looked at me, eyes wide. "Jessica! He can hear you. Don't talk like that."

I stared at her blankly. Was this woman crazy? The babe was short of four weeks old. I mean, I had a hunch he was smart, but I was fairly certain he didn't understand the actual words I was saying. Why in the world did it matter whether I was complaining around him?

I'm now ten years in, and I have learned to expect (and respect) this response from my mom. She is a firm believer that children, babies included, *do* understand more than we give them credit for.

To this day, if I call whining asking a question about one of my children, I know the first thing out of her mouth will be, "Jessica. She can't hear you right now, *can she*?" And I have to pinky swear that the children are out of range before I can vent.

And I'll admit, her belief has sort of rubbed off on me. While I am still guilty of it myself, it bothers me when I hear it in public. The child can be a few months old or about to enter middle school. Even if the kid is within earshot, mothers will say things like:

"She has been a pill today. I don't know what her problem is."
"She keeps waking up every night, screaming and screaming. She's just a horrible sleeper."
"Oh, he's so shy. He's my quiet one."

"She threw the biggest tantrum in Target today. She was so
   naughty!"
"He has been biting people! He's a biter."
"She is not good at sharing."
"I am so fed up with these kids. They have all been terrible
   today."

Honestly, I'm sure that I have said things along these lines
within earshot of my children. Some days, some issues, are just
frustrating. And sometimes seeing another sympathetic adult opens
the floodgates to a giant outpouring of a long day's emotions. I get
it. But I also think we (myself included) need to remember *how
powerful words are.*

I still remember the girl in seventh grade who told me, "You
always smile. I'm going to call you smiley." I still remember my
teacher in fourth grade coming by to comment on what a beautiful
N I had made in cursive. (True story: I waited in vain all year for
her to compliment another letter. Sniff, sniff.) I still remember my
dad telling me I had a knack for connecting with each and every
person in a room. I remember all of these words. I soaked them up.
And I became them. Words are powerful, and even more so from
the adults we look up to and love.

Parents, trust me. I know how positively exasperating raising
little ones can be. They are enigmatic, patience-trying, eardrum-
bursting little creatures sometimes. All of us want our children to
grow up and be pleasant humans. But as we interact with them,
we must watch our words because how we treat them goes beyond
the effect it has on their views of themselves; it models how they
will treat others. If we want them to do it with kindness, then we
must be authentically kind ourselves. How desperately we need the
culture of kindness today. We can grow kids who are kind, and it
starts with us modeling kindness to them.

Why Every Child Should Have a Pet

Last week when I came home from the grocery store, I was greeted at the door with my five-year-old daughter shouting, *"Mom, did you see my lizard? I caught him outside, and he's in the living room!"* I went to the living room and experienced a brief moment of panic when Superstar was nowhere to be found in the box on the piano. Fortunately Superstar possessed a high degree of "caminflauge," as my daughter put it, and was sneakily hiding under some houseplant leaves. Superstar was a midsized gecko that I'm surmising must have been suffering from one ailment or another, given that he was so easily taken into captivity. Not helping his cause was his airtight plastic IKEA bin with the lid snapped shut. I found myself taping plastic wrap over the box and poking holes in it before I had even unloaded the eggs. (File this under "Things You Didn't Think You Would Do As a Mom.")

My daughter loved to pick him up, and wasn't it neat that his eyes did this cool trick where they bulged out when she ~~squeezed~~ held him? She had made a noble effort in decorating his IKEA storage bin with miscellany from the front yard, but I felt fairly certain that his natural habitat was a bit different from the waterless four-by-six-inch plastic bin sitting under the air conditioning vents. In other words, Superstar's days were numbered and dwindling quickly. I didn't want any gecko's blood on my hands, ailing or not. I also didn't want my daughter to freak out when she woke up to a dead lizard. So it was partially selfish, but I said, "Baby, tonight we have to let Superstar go. He needs to live in the grass. Outside. With his friends." (P.S. Geckos are solitary creatures, but I wasn't going to tell her that.)

So that evening I let her take him outside, hold him one last time, and lay him down on the grass to be free. He took off up a shrub, turning around one last time to say, "Thanks, Mom, for saving my life." No, he actually didn't do that last part. Oh my goodness, though, you would not believe the sadness from my little one. Her bottom lip puckered out, tears—real ones—streaming down her cheeks. She collapsed in my arms. "I miss Superstarrrrr!"

Her little, kind, nurturing, compassionate heart had come alive as she cared for and loved this little lizard, even if he was in our home for only seventeen (very cold) hours. It's the power of a pet.

I believe every child should have a pet.

I know some of you reading would glare me down over the pages if you could. *A pet?!* you're thinking. *I hate dogs and I'm allergic to cats! I'm barely keeping the kids alive!* And then there are others of you, from the *Marley and Me* club, who feel as if your dog is basically your firstborn child.

I'm going to go ahead and spoil this out of the gate; the Smartts are dog-less and cat-less. If any of us Smartts are in the same room with a feline for longer than ten minutes, we're projecting snot up and down the walls. I *think* we could tolerate a dog, and I'd love a miniature dachshund (the breed I grew up with), but my husband declares that this adorable breed is actually more a *cat* than a *dog* (insert eye roll here).

So when I say, "Every child should have a pet," I mean this to include all the families reading. The allergics, the clean freaks, the apartment bound, the dog haters and the cat-phobics—the whole gamut of families. Why? Because something happens inside children when they care for animals.

There's actually more to the lizard story. What I didn't tell you yet is that we have two lizards *already* residing within the confines of our home. Yes, two bumpy, spotted, slithery leopard geckos named Stewart and Martin live in the schoolroom in artificially warmed terrariums. (I am waiting for my "Mom of the Year" plaque to arrive.) You would not believe how much these cold-blooded reptiles have snuck into our hearts. That our family could come to know and love two lizards, of all things, proves my point even more.

It took me six months to get up the nerve to touch them, and a year to hold one (those are the actual time periods, not an exaggeration). But now, would you believe I actually find myself sweet-talking these awful creatures when no one is watching? The other day Todd walked by, shocked to see me holding one. I looked up sheepishly and confessed, "He looked like he was cold!"

What if you can't get dogs or cats, and reptiles freak you out? My sister is in this group. For my nephew's birthday they got a slew of goldfish. *I mean, surely*, I thought, *goldfish are the lamest pets ever.* Those poor boys at least need a reptile. And then I heard my nephew talking about his fish. He noted what the fish did when he was afraid and how he liked his tank arranged. This sweet goldfish named Blackeye was precious to my nephews (and fortunately had a longer-than-average life-span, going on three years).

A pet does many things for a child.

- **It provides a friend.** I remember in my awful days of middle school when Tiger, the striped tabby, was my most trusted friend. I had a secret crush on a boy named Alex who, unfortunately, had a not-so-secret crush on my cousin Sheila. Oh, it was the worst! I'd often come home in tears. And then I'd creep to the back porch, find my faithful outdoor cat, stroke his fur and tell him all my woes. Silly as it sounds, the bond we shared encouraged something deep inside of me that helped teach me the importance of being there for someone else.
- **It provides an opportunity to learn responsibility.** Children are used to being cared for, but pets are often the first opportunity for them to be the ones caring for someone or

something else. In our home I often quote Proverbs 12:10: "The righteous care for the needs of their animals," when I am receiving backlash because someone doesn't "feel like" scooping up lizard poop out of the corner of the cage. (I know you are really envious of this life we live.) I have one child who is a born animal whisperer, sensitive to their emotions and needs, and one who talks 99 percent of his waking moments and who doesn't naturally notice anyone's needs, reptile or not. Our pets have been a good training ground on caring for a creature with compassion.

- **And pet ownership provides an opportunity to learn.** Pets help kids learn about nature, up close and personal, through caring for something else in all kinds of arenas: surgeries and stitches, mating, aggression, a mother's nurture for her babies, teeth and beaks and shredded skin and fins and fur.

I never anticipated the part that two lizards would play in the lives of my kids. And I have no regrets about this Facebook Marketplace purchase. Maybe you've been looking for a sign about whether to give your kids a pet. Here it is. Please consider my official vote for "child's best friend" (even if that best friend is not a retriever but a lizard).

P.S. Leopard geckos eat only live crickets. They also shed their skin and eat it. These are two facts I wish I had known before we fulfilled "leopard gecko" from the list for Santa. You're welcome for that information.

We Are Different, but We Can Be Kind

In October 2019, in the very visible press box of the Dallas Cowboys stadium, two famous people chatted. They smiled, they joked, they almost looked as if they liked each other. This wouldn't be unusual or have garnered any attention except for one minor tidbit: these two famous friends were Ellen DeGeneres and former US president George W. Bush. Other than an apparent affinity for professional football, the similarities between these two celebrities would seem to be nonexistent. Ms. DeGeneres is a liberal and outspoken lesbian who hosts a talk show. Former president Bush is a conservative Republican who passed and upheld policies when he was in office that many considered to be anti-LGBT.[1] And yet here they were, sitting side by side, nearly acting like . . . friends.

To me, the crazy part of this event was how people freaked out at this odd but amiable interaction. It was *inconceivable* to most people that you could interact in a civil, even friendly, way with someone who differs so profoundly from you. This is a sad testimony to the state of affairs today. For those of us who are raising kids, this is more than just an interesting story. It says something profound about the world in which our children are living.

If you're reading this book, you might be doing a bunch of stuff differently than the general public. If you raise kids who take technology breaks, enjoy work, love reading, and don't kill themselves on the altar of sports, fashion, and being cool, your family will seem a little weird. There are two important lessons kids need:

1. It's 100 percent okay to be different from my peers.
2. I can be kind and friendly to people who are different from me.

The weird thing is, sometimes kids are better at this than grown-ups. Yes, they notice differences between human beings and are quick to (loudly) point them out. ("Mom, why does that lady have such a big stomach?" one child shouted to me across the bananas at Walmart.) Yet the cool thing is, they also make friends with people who are different from them much more quickly than we adults would.

Friends of ours adopted a young girl from China who has a slight handicap and limps with one leg dragging a bit. As a wannabe doctor, my daughter noticed this physical abnormality right away and had only 732 questions about what the limp was, if the girl had been to the doctor, did it hurt, and so on. Yes, she noticed the difference. But she *loved* playing with this girl. She'd help her along, wait for her if they were running, ask her questions. She was a friend to her.

I would never in my mature grown-up-ness have asked the point-blank questions my daughter did. I would know I "shouldn't." And yet did I get down and play with her? Who was a better friend to her? My daughter. Maybe part of letting them be kids means not interrupting their innocent acceptance with our own long explanations. Maybe letting them be kids means championing that childlike kindness toward those different from us.

Certainly I'm not implying that children are perfect. They can be mean and unkind like the rest of humanity. But the glory of letting them be kids is embracing and encouraging the carefree friendships they develop with all sorts of kids and elderly adults, backyard lizards, and neighborhood dogs. Here are a few ways you might be able to encourage kindness in your children:

- **Open your home.** Our friends Page and Stockton are models of how to open your home to others. Their kitchen, front yard, and trampoline are frequently overflowing with people to love. It might be single moms and their kids from the battered women's shelter. It might be college students for a Bible study or a family they met at school. To Page and Stockton, it doesn't matter how you look, talk, or think. *You are welcome here*. And their kids see this.

- **Sponsor a Compassion child.** This is a tangible way to give your heart and your money to someone profoundly different from you.[2]

- **Teach kindness to those who hurt you.** It's natural to want to hit back, respond with equal cruelty, or repay someone for being a bully. The real treasure comes when we can begin to grow in our children the understanding that those who are cruel often need love the most.

- **Befriend the elderly.** It's not trendy like other causes, but the elderly are one of the most lonely and overlooked segments of society. And they love being with children! Just a simple step of delivering stems of flowers and a card to nursing home residents can make someone's day.

- **Speak truth in kindness.** The idea of kindness *sounds* simple and easy, but it is not simple and it is not always easy. How do you show kindness to a mean playground bully? How can you be friends with someone who talks and jokes in a way that you're not allowed to talk and to joke? In consideration, let's back up to Ellen DeGeneres and George W. Bush. These two public figures exemplify something downright courageous and noble: you can believe what you believe but still be gracious and kind. Truth and love. We're bullied into thinking it's one or the other. But what if it's both?

Don't for one second be afraid for your family to be different, to be yourselves. Stand up for who you are and what you believe.

But do it with kindness. If we can balance this rare and beautiful combination of truth and kindness, we're raising unicorns today—children with conviction but also gentleness.

THE GIFT OF MANNERS AND KINDNESS

but do it with kindness. If we can balance boundaries and beautiful correction of truth with kindness, we've a long runway, endless runway, with correction and also kindness.

CHAPTER NINE

THE GIFT OF FAMILY

Why Kids Need a Tribe and

They Need It to Be You

For about two hours of my life, I was totally cool. This was made possible because I was an unmarried, newly employed, fresh-out-of-college, bright-eyed, ambitious young chick with hours and hours to spend on myself. I had every category of in-style shoe. I frequented the aisles of Target and Anthropologie to refresh my wardrobe. My hair was always highlighted and perfectly curled with this Jessica Simpson backward-curling-iron technique we were all doing. If I turned on the radio, I knew all the words and who was singing. I knew the places we were supposed to go and the activities we were supposed to be doing. I. Was. Cool. It was a wonderful (albeit fleeting) sensation.

Spoiler alert: this was not sustainable. Over the next fifteen years I got bills and got married and got pregnant and got pregnant again and then got really anxious. Normal grown-up jobs, such as researching health insurance plans and unclogging the sink drain, took up my time. In short, I am now that clearly outdated minivan mom I swore I would never be.

Today if I walk in the mall (which I try to avoid because the music gives me a headache), I have to exercise a deliberate amount of self-control not to ogle. Why is everything crop top? Why must everything look so grungy and mismatched? Are those kids really old enough to be groping each other? I am the persnickety, disoriented, outdated mom who walks into the makeup store, finds a hip-looking teenager, and whispers, "Is this lipstick color in style? I have no idea." (Note to moms: I highly recommend this technique. I get tons of compliments on my lipstick.)

One somewhat surprising observation is how little I actually care about this loss of cool. My husband still thinks I'm hot, and there is something incredibly freeing about just giving up and wearing yoga pants and that printed t-shirt from that one race you ran. It's a deep relief to arrive at a level of quiet confidence that adulthood brings.

There's just one little disconcerting problem. I cannot stay in this cozy, cultural hole indefinitely. And neither can you. You may have little kids right now, but I predict that before you know it, one will be towering over you. Our children are rapidly sprinting toward the years of Forever 21 and indie music and Snapchat and other things we don't even know the names of.

I don't know about you, but this makes me very uncomfortable. We need to know more about teen culture—quick. My first safe step was to find someone I trusted who has a pulse on teen life. My friend Cliff Wright is a metro director for Young Life, which excels in its ministry to meet high schoolers where they are, so the leaders are in the arena, working with the animal, the Modern Teenager, itself. They are seeing youth culture at its purest, unadulterated form.

Cliff will know, I concluded. He also has a unique perspective; not only does he know the teenage culture but he's also a dad. Someone who knows the Daniel Tiger potty song and also knows what tenth graders do on apps when their parents aren't looking. *This* is someone worth talking to, I determined. And it was true. Cliff has taught me a ton about teen life.

On our first lesson he scribbled a diagram of the youth culture on the back of a Panera napkin. It was mind-blowing. I mean my brain literally hurt trying to wrap itself around how much things had changed from when I was in school. As Cliff says, parents today think they know what it's like to be a teenager, but most likely they don't. They need to begin by realizing how much they don't know.

As Cliff explained, one profound difference between what we experienced and what our children will experience is that *there was a unified cultural narrative in answer to the question, "Who am I?"* I'm not saying life was easy for everyone in prior years, because that would be silly, but at least we had identity. We knew who we were.

For instance, there was a generally accepted "social ladder," and you knew where you were on it. If you were raised prior to the year 2000, your ladder probably looked something like the following: jocks and pretty girls at the top, the smart kids after that, then maybe the band members, and so on and so forth. The system was clear; you knew where you stood. There was also less confusion on the national scale. We had more of a sense of unity and belonging to our country, where there was a widely accepted narrative (for example, America = good and Communists = bad). Finally, there were generally accepted gender roles. This meant that even if you had a crappy home life or you were at the bottom of the social ladder, at least you had a solid sense of identity in who you were physically, where you fit in socially, and how that all played itself out in the world.

Kids in upcoming generations do not have this. For starters, the national narrative is downright confusing. If I am a kid today, in the year 2020, is President Donald Trump the bad guy or the good guy? Is America inherently good? Or is it bad? And what about gender roles? They have become like scrambled eggs with no discernible form. The answers to these questions aren't the point. The point is, there is no widely accepted answer.

For many kids, the preferred place to find identity is in their friends. As Cliff explains it, instead of the social ladder many of us knew, there are instead pockets of little "tribes" in teenage culture, marked by similar hobbies or traits. These tribes have their own lingo, their own shared values and identity. They tell a kid, *you are valued because you are like us.* What joins them together is a commonality of a music type, a hobby, a sport, or a video game. These tribes are where kids get their sense of self.[1]

If your children are approaching middle school without a grounding sense of who they are, then they will find a group that tells them who they are. In *Hold On to Your Kids*, Gordon Neufeld nails it: "For the first time in history young people are turning for instruction, modeling and guidance not to mothers, fathers, teachers and other responsible adults but to . . . their own peers. . . . They are being brought up by each other."[2]

Kids being brought up by each other? I don't know about you, but I taught junior high; that is an absolutely terrifying thought. There has perhaps never been a greater need for the sense of identity that the family offers. That is a really important sentence, so I am going to say it again. *There has perhaps never been a greater need for what the family offers.*

For a kid to be a kid, he needs a family. Leonard Sax explains that kids can't get the unconditional acceptance and love they so badly need from peers; they can get it only from loving parents.[3] Kids need to know it doesn't matter if everyone makes fun of your glasses, or doesn't invite you to the sleepover, because *you always have us*. (What a tremendous gift to give a fledgling, developing soul in the chaos of adolescence. A gift of people, always and forever *for* you.) Children need the confidence that comes from parents and family who think they're great. (Because we become the words that are spoken over us.) They need a reason to say no. They need fun people doing fun stuff that isn't illegal or dangerous so they have somewhere else to go on Friday night.

We give our kids so much when we give them the stability of an authentic, loving, engaged, and fun family. Did you notice that I didn't have "perfect" in that list? That was on purpose because (take a deep breath) it's okay that your family has issues. All families do. Maybe this "family" essay is making you feel guilty because the one you have is blasé and imperfect. Maybe you thought of your anger or your broken marriage or how you've grown busy and disconnected from things you believe in. There is no perfect family, but you can start right now to make yours stronger. Forget the neighbors', forget mine, forget the one you wish you had. Here are just a few simple ways to give your kids the gift of family:

- **All kinds of traditions.**

    Have many—big ones, little ones, weird ones, even cliche ones. We do the "slow clap" at dinner if someone does something big. Yesterday at dinner I shared that my daughter had learned to swim during her last swim lesson! The boys proceeded to stop eating chili and start the slow clap of recognition. I started to reprimand them (generally being opposed to loud, unmannerly behavior at the table), and then I stopped. This was our thing, I remembered! We do this. It's a funny little thing, our slow clap to tell someone they're awesome. The chili can wait. I wrote a book on traditions called *Memory-Making Mom*, so you can get other ideas there too—other tips to add things that say, "We do this together. It's our thing. We're a family." Here's a great first step: ask your kids what they love that your family always does. *Boom.* Those are your anchors.

• **Shared hobbies.**

We like biking together, cheering for the Virginia Tech Hokies, going to a NASCAR race, laughing at Garfield books, and watching *Dude Perfect*. I know you have your own things you love together. These things mean more than you think they do. They mean as much as the summer camps, picking up the air filters that must be installed in the house, and taking that check to the bank. Take time for your hobbies. It's doing something deep and real on the inside—creating a family!

• **Unconditional love.**

When I was in high school, I was driving all three of my siblings to school when my tire blew and I ran off the road. It's kind of fuzzy, but I definitely have some vague guilt about the incident. Maybe I went off the road and hit something and that's why the tire blew. Maybe I wasn't paying attention as well as I should have been. Maybe I swerved super far off the road. Anyway, when my dad arrived, I definitely had a sheepish, guilty face about the whole thing. He was overwhelmingly gracious. He told me over and over again he knew I did the right thing and he was so proud of me and grateful we were safe. It still makes my throat get all gulpy and emotional to think about how he cheers for us and is on our side. I know it doesn't seem like kids appreciate things like that. I have one who sulks away like a turtle, sheepish and embarrassed, when you tell him how proud you are. But let us not forget what a gift that love is to our kids. They need to know we have their backs, period.

Also, families need to like one another. Yes, not just *love* in an overarching, generic way but really and truly *like* one another. We tell one another that we are "okay" when we really and truly like and accept one another. Do all your kids know that you like them *and* you love them? Sometimes it's work to like them, and I get that. (I can say this because I know it's work to like *me* sometimes too.)

We can't forget how life is vastly different for teenagers today. With so many young adults looking to their friends to learn who they are, we need more than ever to offer them the gift of family for unconditional love, friendship, and identity.

Your Presence Means More to Your Kids Than You Realize

You could not have told us four kids that a better dad existed on earth than our dad. Sadly, he had to be gone quite a bit for work. I remember the ache I would feel on Thursday evenings when I walked into his room to see an open suitcase, him prepping to leave for the weekend NASCAR race where he worked.

It's not that we did specific things with my dad. He did stuff with us, but it wasn't *what he did* that mattered. *It just felt better when he was home.* Everything in the house felt better. It felt like all was right in the world—Dad was home. Just having him around, hearing his voice, smelling his cologne, hearing him cheer when you swished a shot in the driveway basketball hoop.

One weekend I went with him on a work trip to California. Don't ask me what we talked about, where we ate, what we did. I don't remember those things. What I do remember is that I was with Dad. He's one of those people who seems to know everyone and can do anything. Getting whisked around with him—hearing his inside chatter about who we'd met and what he was doing—I just soaked it up. Just being around him was enough.

I remember this and feel a little less resentful when my children (whom I have cared for diligently for over eight hours) rush to the door and give my husband a welcome fit for a prince from a faraway land. He's merely returning home after a day's work, but you'd think he's a celebrity, the fanfare is so great. ("Hey, remember me, kids? I'll be over here if you need me.") I'm only joking; it's a wonderful thing. And I get it. It's just better when Dad's home.

There is such a tremendous lesson here for us parents. There is something to be said for quality time, but there is also something to be said for quantity of time. Kids need a good *quantity* of time with their parents for several reasons:

- **It shows us in our everyday lives, doing ordinary things well.** I learned work ethic watching my mom iron a shirt (so exhaustingly thorough!). I learned kindness hearing her chat patiently with the sweet lady at the dry cleaner's. I watched my dad clean out his car and learned what it looks like to take care of something. (I'm sorry, Dad, I've failed you here with our minivan.) These ordinary moments are where character gets skin and bones. We can read the devotions and give the lectures, but kids do what they see.

- **It builds rapport and trust in the relationship.** Your consistent presence shows kids that they can come to you when they need you, because you will be there. In one of my favorite movies, *It's a Wonderful Life*, young George Bailey sees his boss, a pharmacist, put poison in a medicine capsule. George is concerned but not sure what to do. His eyes land on a sign that says, "Ask Dad. He knows." George drops the medicine and sprints down the street to his dad's office at Bailey Building and Loan. This was always such a tender moment for me. Young George is in a predicament, and he goes directly to Dad. Our children are going to have those moments. They *are having* those moments. They are facing dilemmas and choices, and their world is getting more complicated by the minute. Are we there? And do they know they can run to us?

- **It develops friendship.** *Friendship* isn't a word we typically associate with family, but I believe it is what holds a family together. My siblings and I are all more than thirty years old, but Together is one of our favorite places to be. No one makes us; we like it because we are friends. Friendship is built in the doldrums, the daily mundanity of life. I'll be honest. For the first few years of parenting, it doesn't feel much like you're building a friendship. And maybe you aren't, yet. But then one day you'll make a real joke with your kids and all laugh together. You'll tell them (tears pricking your eyes) about something you're worried about, and you can tell from their faces they care. You'll have a genuine discussion about the refugee crisis, you'll all ride bikes together, and every last one of you will enjoy it. You have begun to build friendship, with time becoming the mortar between the bricks.

- **It matters because authority brings comfort.** In my two-hundred-home neighborhood, 90 percent of the kids congregate in a single cul-de-sac after school—the cul-de-sac with the garage doors open and the parents home. A lot of the kids have freedom to be wherever they want to be. They could roam up to the Exxon station on their motorized scooters if they wanted. They could hide in their basements and play *Madden*. But I'm amazed that they mostly come to the homes where the parents are. This is absolutely fascinating to me. I am not talking about uber-attached preschoolers here. These are junior high boys with nearly limitless freedom, craving independence. Why are they drawn to the houses with thirty-something stay-at-home moms? I think it's comforting to them in a way that is difficult to articulate. There is the surface explanation involving Band-Aids, popsicles, and cups of ice water. But couldn't they secure these things in an uninhabited home? Like lightning bugs to a streetlamp, kids are magnetically drawn to homes with moms who are inside boiling pasta and folding towels.

There's no doubt that kids need time with parents nearby. Parents they can learn from, to find wisdom, to build friendship, and to gain comfort. What does this mean for parents?

When you can, be nearby. When you can't offer them quality time, try for quantity of time. In practical terms this looks like taking kids on your have-to-be-done errands and working from home when you can. Full disclosure: I'm writing this alone from a booth at Panera Bread. So I'm not saying to never leave your kids. But it takes a lot of time to be a mom or dad, and from what the older ladies say at Target when they stop me in the canned beans aisle, we will never regret the time we spend with our kids.

Don't become weary in being a present parent. My kids have this new habit where they say, "Mom?" (Yes?) "I was thinking." (Yes?) "Can I ask you a question?" (Yes.) And they finally ask the question. I don't know if any of you have been in "brain cell survival mode." In that state, minimal questions are preferred. This is nonsense language to a kid; they have no framework to understand it. They can ramble meanderingly about what the cat did outside, their dream last night, how to build a fantasy football team, et cetera, et cetera, forever. Keep being there, even when it is exhausting! You're doing the right thing.

In baseball there are all these funny-to-me chants you say to kids on the ball field. One of them is, "Way to be ready!" This cracks me up because you're kind of just praising them for standing there. In the same way, parent, this is your equivalent pep talk. "Way to be ready, Mom! Way to be ready, Dad!" Way to be there. It means more than you'll ever know.

On Being Present When
Your Kids Play

I remember well the young mom stage. This was the stage in which you literally could not pee without praying that everyone would be alive by the time you washed your hands. This was the stage I had to call the poison control center *three times in two months* because my toddler daughter (daughter!) attempted to guzzle a bottle of baby Advil (my fault), rubbed tea tree oil on her lips (my fault), and potentially ingested some of her brother's slime that had the corrosive borax cleaning solution in it (also basically my fault). I was legitimately afraid that after a certain number of calls to the state poison control hotline, they move your file to the authorities to investigate. There were some extreme levels of mom guilt over these incidents.

The point is, there is a time in parenting when you Can. Not. Turn. Your. Back. If you want to have a playdate in the neighborhood during this stage, here is how you do it. You get everyone dressed in seasonally appropriate clothing. (Someone will violently protest being dressed for the actual weather conditions.) Then you line up their waters and your waters and your coffee and their other pairs of clothes and the Special Items You Don't Go Anywhere Without. These items will vary kid to kid, stage to stage. I had one with a very close attachment to a fuzzy burp cloth, and one to pieces of PVC pipe . . . we thought for a long time he was destined to be a plumber. Once you've got all your stuff, you start putting people in the right vehicles to transport them. Maybe you have a little red car with a long handle. Perhaps you have the double stroller situation. Likely you've got one bound and determined to "drive myself" on some sort of scooter or bicycle—which is fine as long as you've left forty-five minutes early.

When you get to where you're going, you will probably have . . .

let's see . . . five minutes and twenty-nine seconds available for actual adult interaction, so if you have topics you need to discuss, you better make it snappy. The rest of the visit will be occupied by

1. keeping your kids safe,
2. keeping your kids safe, and
3. that's basically it.

These were the years of playdates when my sisters and I would have to camp out in different quadrants in the yard. "Okay, I've got the front yard. Who's got the back?" And we'd shout other things like, "Do you think that's dangerous?" "Can anyone see the girls?" "Is that sound crying or laughing?" "Why are they all wet?" "Is that water or pee?" "Is that poop or mud?"

We owned only two plastic brown Adirondack yard chairs, but one or both were always empty; someone was always running around, fishing something dubious out of a toddler's mouth, pushing someone on a swing ("Higher! Higher!"), or breaking up a fight over the Little Tikes Coupe (this is the product Rachel Jankovic aptly termed "the sin wagon" because whoever played with it quickly became naughty).[4]

And this is your life for a while. But then at some point in the future, and it is quite gradual, you will one day be sitting in your house and realize, "My kids are playing. And I'm not watching them." And it will feel okay, and it will feel really weird, all at the same time. The next time you have a playdate, you realize you can all sit (sit!) in the same spot and have an actual conversation lasting more than five minutes and twenty-nine seconds. You won't even know what to talk about.

Then a little bit later (but, again, you hardly realize it's happened), there comes a day when a child will say, "Can I go to _____'s house to play?" And you say, "Okay."

(Pause for a moment of commemoration and silence for this tremendous parenting rite of passage.)

It is tempting to get really, really comfortable with this stage. Freedom. Peace. Quiet. Alone time.

But kids still need you around, even when they're not eating dirt. They don't need you in the same emergent way as before. They've mostly mastered Not Standing Underneath a Moving Swing and other such lifesaving skills. But they still need you around.

First of all, I want to explain what *I do not mean* by kids "need you around."

You don't need to hover. I do not mean that we have to hang around our elementary and middle school kids like a brooding mother hen, watching and managing every second. On the contrary, independence is a crucial experience for growing children (see chapter 2).

You don't have to be the counselor. I don't mean that kids should never work out their squabbles and conundrums among themselves.

So then what *do* they need us for? How can we parent them well during this stage of newfound independence for all?

We can give them a pep talk. I don't mean a long lecture. I mean stepping into their world and reframing what is happening, telling them a story, inspiring them to a different way of thinking, and helping them to make good choices in their real lives. I don't give one of these talks every day; it's more like a once-a-month thing. But the point is, you need to be around (or regrouping afterward, at dinner or whatever) to understand what your kids are living through. A lot of stuff is happening during interactive play. As your kids are out there playing Mommy and baby, managing a mud kitchen, or competing in yard baseball, real-life issues are coming up: how we treat one another, whether we are honest or not, what language is appropriate. I don't know about your kids, but my kids aren't going to notice or be able to handle these issues on their own. None of the children I have observed are going to say, "Guys, hang on a minute. We aren't really demonstrating good stewardship of the earth by utilizing this entire roll of paper towels to pretend-blow our noses." Or "Just a second. As one of the older kids, I'm not being a good example of servant leadership. Maybe I should be less bossy." And it would be overkill to make every playdate into a life lesson, but as you hop in and out of their play, every so often you'll get the nudge to talk with them about what's happening. These junior TED Talks are inspirational, not guilt inducing. They are relational, not preachy. Don't get me wrong; there's a time and place for barging outside and ordering everyone to stop washing the minivan with Brillo pads, *right this second*. But the interventions I'm referring to here are different. They're kind and pastoral. You can talk to your kids all the livelong day about honesty and kindness and fairness, but if you really want to make a dent, find a real-time application during play.

We can make sure they're not doing something reckless to life or personal property. Listen. Maybe your kids are a different species from mine, but sometimes mine do things that—how do I put this—exhibit less-than-ideal judgment? Do you know any children who free-fall from the top of the minivan, or climb up a ladder onto the roof? I have seen it happen. Sometimes just a mere appearance from the garage: "Oh, hey there. I'm just taking out the trash bag. Hope you guys are having a great day!" can make the difference between an ER visit and not an ER visit.

We can provide food and water. At first glance this sounds like the least important of all of them, but do you know any children who get "hangry" (hungry + angry = hangry)? I have a nephew who collapses into a puddle when he needs a snack. Once he reaches this point, any chance of productive play is shot to smithereens. I can be inside innocuously doing the dishes, and I'll hear the moaning and weeping that are the distinct sounds of Tommy being hungry. Give him a granola bar, and he's back at it. It's tempting to get nice and cozy with the independence, but children cannot play for hours on end with no sustenance. I mean they can, but there will be repercussions, some of them dangerous. We provide the fuel for our children's play, stepping in with cups of icy lemonade on a hot day, a round of oranges or cookies at the end of a flag football game, some hot chocolate and fresh socks during a snow day.

I love the way Susan Schaeffer Macaulay put it: "[Children] need privacy from intruding adults, but they need interested support in quarrels, thinking of another way around a problem, providing food, and, at the end, bringing the children tactfully back into the world where supper is ready, the camp has to be packed up, children are tired and ready for the soothing routine of evening stories."[5]

By all means, mom of older children, enjoy that uninterrupted cup of coffee. Have a blast making dinner without someone crushing your ankles with a baby walker. But don't forget it: your kids still need you around.

CHAPTER TEN

THE GIFT OF INNOCENCE

The Blessing of Not Being a Grown-Up

I once asked my four-year-old, "Do you want apples or grapes?" My mother-in-law, who had accumulated a large lump of common sense with children from her days of being a kindergarten teacher, put her arm on me and smiled encouragingly. "It is so good that you said that. Some parents will open the refrigerator and say, 'What do you want for dinner tonight?' They have no idea that they are completely overwhelming their child. Kids can't make those big decisions. Their little brains aren't ready for that. Give them two choices, and then let them decide. The kids think they are being independent, but it's happening in a way their little brains can manage."[1]

We sense from the grumbling we sometimes receive that our little independent beings want to be the ones making decisions. They do, and they should. But *little ones*—about grapes or apples, this shirt or that. Their minds are easily overwhelmed and therefore incapable of deciding between too many options or making decisions that are too important. One of my favorite lines is "I'd like to have your opinion about something, but I want you to know that I'll be the one making the decision." My kids know their opinions matter, but they also know (to their deep-down relief) that they aren't the ones who have to have the final say.

It is a burden to a child to have to decide adult things. *Where should we live? Where should I go to school?* Even if it feels like they want to decide these things, they're inwardly relieved that there is a grown-up at the wheel. They want you to take the reins on the tough decisions. This means two things for us parents:

1. Someone else has to be the grown-up.
2. That someone is you.

Modern parents struggle to do this well. As Leonard Sax states,

> Here's what's weird. We parents are spending more and more time and money on parenting, but when you look at the results, things are getting worse, not better. . . . Here's my diagnosis. Over the past three decades, there has been a massive transfer of authority from parents to kids. Along with that transfer of authority has come a change in the valuation of kids' opinions and preferences. In many families, what kids think and what kids like and what kids want now matters as much or more than what their parents think and like and want. . . . These well-intentioned changes have been profoundly harmful to kids.[2]

Grown-ups make hard decisions. And *grown-ups carry difficult knowledge and concerns that kids should not have to carry.* When I was in sixth grade, my mom told us kids that my dad had lost his job, but not to worry because he would get a new one. That is actually the end of the story because that's about the extent of the knowledge I have about it. I remember being vaguely antsy until he was rehired three months later. I remember it being a little odd that I got only one gift for my birthday. But it was a magic set, and it was really cool, and I still got my strawberry Jell-O cake that we always had, and life went on. I don't doubt that it was a load for both of my parents to carry. But would it have helped me or hurt me to have shared in all their worries and fears? I am glad I knew the basics. I am glad I was able to pray. But they carried the heavy load, and mine was a smaller, child-sized load.

In *Simplicity Parenting: Using the Extraordinary Power of Less to Raise Calmer, Happier, and More Secure Kids*, Kim John Payne advises simplifying your home for the health of the child, including clutter, schedules, rhythm, and, finally, "filtering out the adult world."[3]

Dr. Payne poignantly asks,

> Do you have any childhood memories of being in the backseat of the car at night, perhaps dozing, while your parents drove through rain or snow, talking quietly in the front seat? . . . The feeling was one of being cocooned and watched over in the darkness. There were distant concerns in the darkness and the weather, concerns perhaps even in whatever they were talking about, but all was well. How wonderful that they knew where to go and how to get there. How comforting that they would deliver you through the dark night, whatever it might bring. And when you got home . . . they might even carry you all the way to bed.[4]

"It is a misnomer," Dr. Payne continues, "to think that we are 'sharing' with our children when we include them in adult conversations with adult concerns. . . . Too much information does not 'prepare' a child for a complicated world; it paralyzes them."[5]

Okay, but what about the issues your children are already facing? It's a broken world. What about racism, abortion, divorce, death that they may have been exposed to? We cannot shield our kids from all of the pain and hurt in the world. Many of you reading have suffered incredibly in your family—struggles that I will never understand or know. How do you protect childhood during these difficult things?

I'm not a child psychologist or expert in this field, but I can offer a few general guidelines, many of which I imagine those of you who have weathered difficulties are already doing.

- **Don't hesitate to consult with a counselor to help your child process hard things in a healthy way.** I feel grateful that over the last decade or so the stigma about counseling and mental health is beginning to lift. It shouldn't feel odd or desperate to see a counselor or to take our children to one. I remember the first time I entered a counselor's office fifteen years ago. I scanned the parking lot with sweaty palms. I prayed no one I knew would be in the waiting room. I slid in and out furtively, completely ashamed. I don't feel this sense of shame anymore. Counseling can be incredibly helpful, and if our children are struggling to process some of the issues they've been forced to carry, a counselor is an excellent step.

- **Provide child-sized explanations, not adult-sized ones.** A friend of mine had to tell her kids that their grandparents were separating. Instead of needlessly giving all the gory details, she wisely said something more appropriate. "Grandma and Grandpa have done some things to hurt each other, so they are going to live apart for a while to work on some things."

- **Don't use them as your sounding board or make them carry your burdens.** I struggle with anxiety. I have shared a little of this with my kids, and I think that's a good thing. For example, sometimes when we say our prayers at night, I will say, "Please help me not to be worried, and please remind me that you will take care of us." But there's a limit to what is appropriate. I'm a verbal processor, so when I'm anxious, I like to talk through (and through and through) all the things I am worried about and have people tell me I don't need to be worried about them. (Moment of silent appreciation for my husband and my mom.) I'll admit that sometimes in a dark moment I just want to vomit the whole thing on my poor, unsuspecting ten-year-old. My worries feel so heavy. But that would be unkind. I do understand that as children grow, the seesaw begins to even, and we can let them carry more and more weight. But it should be tempered with a respect for what they can handle.

Adulthood comes soon enough, with all the responsibilities, decisions, sorrows, and burdens that it brings. Even if it seems as though kids want to decide everything, to know everything, to control everything, *they don't*. So we take on that hard role. In the following essays I'm going to address four particular areas in which we can protect our kids and give them the sweet relief of knowing, "There is a grown-up around, and it is not me."

The One About Sleepovers and Being the "No" Parent

When I was seventeen, I broke up with my longtime boyfriend, Tommy. Tommy was a wonderful guy. My parents, sisters, and brother had become quite attached to him, and it was hard on everyone when it ended. (Note for my husband: But I am so glad it did! Now I have you. Don't get mad that Tommy made it into the book, okay?) Although Tommy was a good guy, I had hunches all along that he was not the one I wanted to marry. (See, Todd?) One night during the summer of our junior year, I tried to break up with him. We talked and cried on the phone for three hours about Teenage Love Stuff. I sat in my bathroom on the toilet cover with wads of snotty tissues littering the floor and thought one thing, full force: *Why didn't my parents keep this from happening?*

I find it so curious that I thought this. I guess you could explain it by saying I had misplaced anger (typical teenager), but I think there was more to it than that. You see, I *knew* to my core my mom and dad were loving parents who took their responsibilities seriously. They often made rules, and although I hated some of those rules, I knew deep down that they were there for our good. When my dating life went terribly wrong, I felt hurt and angry at my parents. All of the nausea and heartbreak I was feeling—if my parents had made rules against dating, I wouldn't be feeling any of that.

This isn't about teenage dating. It's not an indictment of my parents. They balanced grace and rules well, and I know whatever they did was prayerful and intentional.

But the principle is that kids *expect you to protect them*. Of course they may not agree with every rule and boundary. And that's because they don't know what they don't know . . . not until they're sitting on a toilet for a chair sobbing their brains out.

So back to sleepovers—the subject of this essay. I don't think they're the devil, but I do believe this is one area where today's parents have not fully weighed the risks and the rewards. I believe we can protect our kids from a bunch of unnecessary junk by rethinking the sleepover option.

If sleepovers are just one of your nonnegotiables, and you're going to get all hot and bothered reading this chapter, then skip it. We can still be friends. Maybe you want to read it to see just how weird I really am. Whatever the case, remember one thing: *you can change the rules as a parent.* No policy is permanent. If you rethink sleepovers (or anything!) and want to make changes, you can! Parents are allowed to say, "I messed up. I thought I was doing what was right, but I have new information now. I understand you're upset, and you're allowed to be upset, but this is how things will be."

I get that sleepovers have their own nostalgic charm. I remember sneaking trays of nachos at 11:00 p.m., recording silly videos on the camcorder, fishing out the mouse my dachshund threw up in my sleeping bag when we were watching a movie (okay, that is not so charming of a memory).

So I realize they can be fun, but for our family the pros of sleepovers don't outweigh the cons. Childhood sexual experimentation is happening at epidemic proportions, early and among both genders. I could tell you stories about how people thought others parented like they did—but the unfettered access to an iPad, the porn stashed in the bathroom, the Showtime channel streaming on the TV, the sexually violent video games, the lax standards on teenage liquor—these things tell a different story.

So we just say no to sleepovers, and, yes, this can be awkward. It's not fun to wonder if other parents think you're a weirdo or holier-than-thou. It's not fun to have a kid feel disappointed.

But I've learned something from having a child with severe food allergies that has helped me with parenting in general: to define my *most important thing*. Sometimes, for example, a well-meaning friend will suggest something that isn't safe for my allergy kiddo. My friend may say, "Hey, can you guys come over for a giant birthday party with all the foods your kid is allergic to and trampolines and wrestling and food fights?" Deep down, I know that this scenario isn't safe for my kid with the allergies. It's not worth the risks involved, and I see that, crystal clear. But I suddenly feel all hot and conflicted inside. I don't want to hurt her feelings. I don't want to make my son sad. I don't want him to miss out. I don't want it to be awkward. Help!

Then one day I realized, "The most important thing is my son's safety. It is more important than all the other stuff I feel, or anyone else feels. My friend's feelings, my son's friend's feelings, the feelings of anyone else in the world who may not understand: all of those are not as important as keeping my son alive."

When I finally put that into words, it made decisions one thousand times easier. I have already determined the Most Important Thing. Yes, there will be fallout, but I have preemptively decided the fallout is worth it—worth keeping my precious son alive and well. It's worth the rest of the crap I may have to deal with.

Here's another way to put it. In college we played a lot of Spades, the card game. In the game of Spades, the ace of spades is the absolute trump. It doesn't matter how good a card anyone else plays—when you triumphantly lay down the ace of spades, everything else fades away. When we make decisions for what our kids can do, *our kids' well-being is that ace of spades*. It is the trump. There are many other cards with high values, but when you lay down that trump, the other cards pale in comparison to the ace of spades—the job we've been given to care for our children.

"But wait!" you might say. Is our kids' health and well-being *really* the ace? Or is something else more important? What about being kind to others? Being a good friend? Serving the community?

I'm about to say the hardest thing I've had to say in the whole book, but it needs to be said. Yes, we should be kind, and we should be doing good things for our community. But placing our children in situations they cannot handle in the name of being kind to others is not truly kind. You would never, ever armor up your seven-year-old daughter and place her on the front lines of a military battle. We would never do that. It would be cruel and uncaring. Yet there are many situations that our children's hearts and minds are too small and too unready to face.

Back to the sleepovers or any hard decision: *we have to decide ahead of time* what is our ace of spades, then play that card and never mind the others. Whatever hard decision you may need to make, do not be afraid. You be the parent. Your kids will thank you later.

Teaching Your Kids About Sex

The first ten years of parenting were blissful and full of innocence. Oh, we had issues, but they usually involved things like who got the last cookie or people saying "potty words" at lunch or allegations that someone "stole sitting in the gray chair when I went to the bathroom" (gray chair = highly coveted swivel recliner that is the bane of my existence).

One night when we (the kids and I) were eating hamburgers (Todd was working late), my nine-year-old son broke the chewing silence with, "Mom, the last time we played with Danny [not his real name], he asked us if we wanted to touch each other's penises."

The world stopped.

I managed to swallow the bite of hamburger I had been enjoying previously. I remember thinking, *You have to be calm. Do not overreact. Just get more information.*

I said one word: "Wow." Which, if you know me, *was* being calm and not overreacting. It bought me some time to gather my thoughts. I felt nauseated and hot. "Buddy," I said, "what did you say?"

"Oh, we told him that was dumb and we wouldn't do it. He told us we should just pretend to go to the bathroom and all go in there and do it. He did it with his friends."

I imagine you have your own version of this moment, and if you don't, you will. Yours may be much earlier than mine. Homeschooling bought us a few years, I believe. Your scenario may be more terrible and heartbreaking, but it will happen—the moment when innocence dies. It was a wake-up call for us.

I've realized the first great step in preparing kids for sexual purity is this: you talk to them about sex, talk to them early, and keep talking. For a long time I had a nagging gut feeling it was time to talk to our kids. And by had a "gut feeling," this meant I said to my husband in that urgent tone of voice he has come to love, "Babe. You have to teach the boys about sex like ASAP!"

Truthfully, we'd both been putting it off: halfway because we had no clue what words to say and halfway because we dreaded questions like the one my aunt got from my cousin. They lived on a horse farm, so she used the animal mating behavior they'd witnessed to bridge the gap about human procreation. My little cousin was quiet for a while, thinking about the horse mating he'd seen around the farm. "Well, Mom? Who's on top? You? Or dad?" That conversation went dead in a nanosecond.

Questions like that sounded like a lot of fun to us, which means the sex talk went on that list of Things We Really Need to Get To, right up there next to the tax return and replacing the shutter that fell off last spring in the mini tornado. Which is to say, we kept putting it off.

And we probably would have kept putting it off if that incident with the friend hadn't taken place. Todd took that opportunity to talk to the boys, aged seven and nine, about making wise choices and that private parts are private. We hadn't yet explained how babies are made. And if you're curious, that is way too old to wait before talking about sex. Do what I say, not what I do.

We knew that the sex talk was the next step. It felt like we'd already addressed a lot, and we all were still kind of reeling from the incident, so we were biding our time.

A few weeks later I walked upstairs to see one of my sons play-wrestling with my toddler daughter. Still a bit tender from the earlier incident, I took my son aside and kindly reminded him that even when we're playing, we don't touch other people's private parts. He started crying, sobbing uncontrollably. All kinds of thoughts went through my head—what had him so emotionally distraught? It took him forever to say what was bothering him. Eventually he choked out, "Mom, I just don't understand. Why would God have made that?" (Made what?) "Made our private parts. Because they just get us in trouble!"

I am not a crier. But I cried. I felt so, so awful. I felt I had gone about this whole sex thing completely wrong. We had not gotten in front of things and laid a good foundation for God's good plan for sex. Because of that we were playing catch-up and putting out fires, and thus my poor son was all guilty about having his own set of private parts.

I took a deep breath, and for the first time in this whole story, I get to tell you that I did the right thing. I remembered that it's never too late for God, and he is always here. So I prayed, right there, sitting in my master bathroom, next to the empty bottle of bubble bath. "God, help."

And then I started talking. "Buddy," I said, "I need to tell you something. There is a really, really good reason that God made our private parts. And I will tell you that right now. Would you like to know?"

The relief that broke into his face was palpable.

I stumbled through the whole stinkin' thing, no dry runs, no rehearsing, no plan. Thank the Good Lord—my sweet son was *beyond grateful* just to understand. He was nearly giddy with relief. And he had understood, at least as much as someone who had just lost his front tooth could understand. He understood that God had a plan and it was good.

So don't do what I did. From the get-go, lay a foundation of good and beautiful and God's plan. Please, if you haven't, start this very day. Teach them these things:

- God is good.
- God made our bodies and all of them are good.

- Some parts are private.
- There's a very special job for these private parts, and we get to use them when we get married.
- It's a good plan.

One book that is helpful at the early stage is the picture book *God Made All of Me*, by Justin and Lindsey Holcomb. Later, when you get to the age where you will need to explain, you know, the details, I recommend two resources:

- *The Talk: 7 Lessons to Introduce Your Child to Biblical Sexuality*, by Luke Gilkerson
- *God's Very Good Design*, by Mary Flo Ridley

We've now covered two essential things: (1) God made our bodies unique and good and special and (2) God's plan, in basic terms, for sex and marriage. You have laid an excellent foundation. In the 1960s you'd be good to go for a good long while. But there was no YouTube or TikTok in the 1960s, so you do not have the luxury of being silent. You get the privilege of beginning to protect your children's hearts in the modern age. And this brings us to the next step.

How and Why to Porn-
Proof Your Home

Recently I attended a seminar on technology and families, in which the speaker relayed the story of an eighth-grade boy who was addicted to pornography. Evidently this boy threw his phone on the floor, looked at his mom, and said, "I hate you."[6]

This is profound and deeply disturbing. Here was a child suffering in the throes of an intense addiction to pornography who was directing intense rage at his parents. Why? While not all children would necessarily respond this way, it seems this child felt that his parents could have in some way prevented or helped him in his addiction. He wanted them to step up and protect him.

This story makes me feel sad and uneasy. But I am not telling this story to lay a bunch of vague guilt and ambiguous fear on us as parents. On the contrary, I want to motivate us to protect our children today by doing *three specific things*. These three practices can have a tremendous impact on our kids' future sexual integrity.

Pornography is not something I like to think about. For most of my parenting I have been hovering in a little hopeful hole, pretending that my kids are still sitting in Bumbo chairs and eating mashed bananas that I spoon-feed them. I prefer to live in denial because pornography is not fun to think about.

But we must think about it. We must accept that our kids will likely see pornography, and probably earlier than we expect. Many children are exposed to pornography before age ten, and some of them are accessing it regularly by that point.[7]

What can we do to help our children in this area? We are not powerless. I want to encourage parents to consider three practices.

- Practice 1

   Prepare your kids for the moment that they will see porn, arming them with clear steps. We can't be figuratively or literally choking on our hamburgers when the moment comes. We must be ready, and our kids must be ready. How do we do prepare them? One excellent resource is the picture book *Good Pictures Bad Pictures*, which explains what pornography is and what to do when you see it.[8] Have a conversation with your kids. The great thing is that you can have this conversation at any age, even if you feel behind. I've heard people say it's great to talk about this while riding in the car, because eye contact is minimal, which makes it easier to process and talk comfortably.

   Here's what I said. "Kids, I want to talk to you about something. This is kind of a serious thing. You're not in trouble, but I want to tell you something. There are some bad people in the world. Sometimes they make bad pictures. They might take them with their cameras, or draw them like a cartoon, but the pictures show something that's inappropriate: people without all their clothes on. Have you ever seen a picture like this? Maybe on a commercial or on a phone or in a movie?"

   Then allow a long space to answer. Your number one goal in this conversation is to open the dialogue. You're simply giving them a space to share and to set the precedent that this is a safe space. *Just listen.*

   After allowing the kids time to answer (which they may or may not do), continue with, "It might make you feel kind of weird inside when you see pictures like this. That's okay. Here is what I want you to do. Go get an adult right away and say, 'I think you should see this.' Guys, you are not in trouble. Just come get Mom or Dad or another grown-up. Can you remember what to do?"

Then review the steps. It doesn't need to be a thirty-minute lecture (nor should it be), although if they are wanting to talk, answer as many questions as they have. This is a conversation you don't have once, or twice, but regularly. Sometimes if it's been a while, I'll remind my husband, "Go talk to the kids again. It's about time." And he knows what I mean. Just keep going back and reminding them. "Remember that conversation we had about pictures that aren't appropriate? Have you seen any of those recently?" Be somewhat nonchalant so that it's not an epic ordeal to them.

I read an article that suggested that parents of teenagers come up with a code word that teenagers can say and their parents will immediately come and get them from an undesirable situation, no questions asked.[9] This is brilliant for many reasons.

Perhaps you could choose a word or phrase for your kids regarding pornography. Then explain that the word means, "I saw something inappropriate." It's terribly weighty to carry the angsty guilt and discomfort from seeing pornography. You are providing your kids with the easiest possible way to lay down that burden.

- Practice 2

Take specific steps to delay the porn exposure as long as you possibly can. As Melanie Hempe says, pornography changes a developing child's brain. For this reason, the race against pornography is like a premature baby and a mother on bedrest. Every minute in the womb is precious for healthy development. So, too, every minute of childhood is precious. Melanie says, "Give me one more day with them, to attach to our family, to do that list of fun stuff."[10]

Yes, they will eventually see pornography, but do whatever you can to delay those exposures for as long as you possibly can.

How do you accomplish this? It might mean taking away a cell phone. Maybe it's restricting access to a device so it can be used only when your kids are in the living room or other common space. Maybe it's not allowing them to visit a certain friend's home where technology use is not well controlled or telling other parents your kids aren't allowed to be on screens. Maybe it means installing Internet control options. (In fact, this is an absolute must.)

As I write this, Covenant Eyes is a good program. I encourage you to do the hard work and research a good program for you. If you were buying a new car or a vacuum, you'd read the reviews and do the hard work to figure out the best option. Give your kids' hearts the same attention. Do the work to find a good option to guard your home from pornography.

All of the practices I've described are time-consuming, complicated, and potentially awkward. *But there is literally next to nothing you can do in your parenting journey that has the same power to impact their well-being.* You are doing the good work when you guard against pornography addictions. You are giving your kids a fighting chance at healthy sexuality and a childhood filled with LEGOs, and baseball, and Barbies, and not hovering in a basement with guilt over an adult-sized addiction.

- Practice 3

Be open, grace-filled, and authentic, and model repentance. In short, be the kind of someone who you would want to come to if you were struggling with something.

When I need to repent of something, two people I can bring myself to talk to are my prayer triad partners. When I am ashamed, they model grace and love. They hold up my head, and they don't flaunt my secrets. I have seen them confess their own junk. They don't act like they're perfect. It's a little different with a friend versus a child, but the same traits are needed. I want to be a safe place for them to come. Guilt is a heavy burden to bear alone. Nearly impossible, in fact. Give your children the blessed relief of having a place to dump the heavy baggage of guilt and pick up forgiveness in its place. Be that person for them.

You have incredible power to take steps to protect your home from pornography. You have the power to equip your children to know what to do when they see pornography. You have the power to be a safe place for them to come.

Bring Back the Good
Kids' Programing

I have friends who gave all of their TVs away. Every last one. No streaming anything on any device. Justin said, "I really don't miss TV. I thought I would, but it's been great. We find a ton of stuff to do!" Half of me thought it was ridiculously cool, and half of me thought, *No sports . . . ever? No* Madam Secretary *when the kids are in bed?*

I really admire my friend's bravery, and I feel a little jealous. As I've said before, I'm not totally anti-TV. But do you know one thing I am against? Television shows for preteens. They are almost unequivocally awful. And do you know what's *even worse* than preteen shows? Ones that are supposed to be for little kids but are actually preteen shows in disguise. I'll give you just one example. Have you ever watched *Barbie: Life in the Dreamhouse?* Last summer we were on vacation when my daughter was in one of those "if something desperate doesn't happen, I will fall asleep at 3:30 p.m. and sleep for twelve hours" moods that tend to happen on the third or fourth day of vacation. I saw the Barbie show in the Netflix lineup and thought it sounded innocuous enough to pass a little time. My daughter loves Barbie dolls, as most four-year-olds do. This would be a perfect show to keep her awake, right?

Wrong.

Unlike the typical four-year-old, Barbie's favorite things include fashion shows, shopping for accessories with her BFFs, cutting-edge fashion, and dating boys. Here is a sample of the "problems" Barbie faced in some of the episodes:

- Before going on a date with Barbie, Ken tries out a new shampoo that is guaranteed to add maximum volume, but it ruins his look. After bottles and bottles of hairspray, his hair is perfect and ready for his date. (Phew! We dodged a bullet there, Ken!)

- Oh no! Barbie's closet is at maximum capacity. Her friends help her find places to dump her super-stylish leftover clothes.
- Barbie is invited to a party by her "frenemy," who intentionally tells her it's formal attire while it was really *casual*. (*Gasp!*) Barbie is humiliated.

Listen, there is nothing intrinsically wrong with this stuff. I like going on dates and shopping for bathing suits. But I am a grown woman. Why in the world would five-year-olds need to be exposed to crises involving mismatching clothing, bad haircuts, and cheating boyfriends? Spoiler alert: they do not! In the show I mentioned, and so many more, the characters are full of catty insults, millennial acronyms, and drama about boys. It often feels like watching a cartoon version of the Kardashian drama. I wish my example of preschool teledrama were an isolated one, but unfortunately it is not. There are many shows whose target market is young children but whose language, content, and themes are geared for teenagers.

How do you find good content? New things come out every day that your kids will see in the queue and want to watch. It might sound obvious, but a lot of times you have to watch stuff *with* them. You can't trust Netflix ratings. You can't trust what their friends have watched and loved. I do access Common Sense Media, Dove. org, and PluggedIn.com, but you can't find every show or movie on these databases. Even if something looks great, it might not be. Sometimes you just have to watch it with them to see what the deal is. You can't assume something is fine and walk away. I'm guilty of this in a busy moment, but it usually comes back to bite me.

It's hard to find quality entertainment, so you may need to widen your search options. Don't disregard shows that seem to be "childish." A good story is a good story is a good story. Whether you're talking books or movies, if a piece is well done, any age can enjoy it. Practically this means you can let go of the concerns of showing "kiddie" movies to your older children, if you show something that is high quality.

Here's an example. My kids were sick last month, and I wanted to show an afternoon movie. I was scanning all the places but feeling disappointed with the options. All the good ones we'd already watched. My sister suggested *The Aristocats*. At this point my oldest kids are ten and eight, and they are boys. I was doubtful they'd be entertained by a forty-year-old cartoon about girly-looking cats. Oh my goodness! I'm delighted to say I was wrong.

There were literal hoots and howls in the room at parts of this movie. They acted it out for days, told us the jokes, begged to watch it again and again. (And they were sick, and I'd rented it for thirty days, so I said, "What the heck? Sure.") They loved this movie because it was a thoughtful, genuinely funny, well-done piece of entertainment. It didn't matter that it was about cartoon cats. Give some older well-done family movies a chance. If you've become accustomed to the modern movies with snide remarks and adult themes, it may take a second to snap out of it. But your tastes can adjust. Be okay with some eye-rolling and groans in the process. If that's the only option you present, they will come around.

CHAPTER ELEVEN

THE GIFT
OF FAITH

Grace for Kids (and Parents)

Who Mess Up

One night my husband and I were washing dishes. Usually we
don't talk when we are washing dishes; we are in a groove,
completely exhausted, or have nothing left to say. Sometimes
we'll say other sweet things to each other, like "Did you wash this
pan?" or "I have a lump on my elbow, and I think it's a tumor."
(Clarification: Only I ever say these kinds of things. Todd never
notices lumps on his elbows.)

One night I was chewing on some of the things in this book,
feeling uncharacteristically deep and conversational for nine at
night. "You remember when you were in high school, dating girls?"

Todd looked up at me, obviously very nervous as to where this
was heading.

"What I mean is," I continued, "what was it that kept you from having sex? I keep thinking about our boys growing up one day, being nineteen, alone in a dorm room . . . *what do you call that thing* that will make them not want to just sit on their phones looking at porn or to be drunk all the time or whatever? What is *that thing* that makes kids make good choices?"

Deep thoughts for a Tuesday evening washing dishes, like I said. I guess what I was realizing is this: I have all sorts of clever parental precautions and protections posted all around our home. But one day I will no longer be there. My rules will no longer be there. At this point it will be clear what my kids are really made of.

So what is that deep-down trait that helps them make good choices when no one else is watching or punishing or rewarding?

What is *that* called?

Todd shook the water off the bowl he was washing. "I think for me it was the belief that God's ways are really right. I guess I trusted that if I did what he said, things would be better in the end."

I kept thinking about how Todd said that: "If I did what he said, things would be better in the end." What he was essentially describing was faith, believing in something you cannot see.

I know that many of you picked up this book because the theme of capturing childhood spoke to your heart. The virtues of adventure and innocence and play—these things resound deeply in your soul. You want this for your family! You want your kids to be kids! You've nodded your head to much of this, laughed at some, but now we're at the faith part and maybe a few of you are thinking, *Why did she have to go and ruin it with this?* I want you to know that I fully realize that not all of you agree with, or see the need for, a chapter on faith. It seems irrelevant, misplaced, unnecessary.

If you are one of those people, *we can still be friends.* I mean it. I used to only have friends who were exactly like me, and that meant I had precisely two of them, and life was really bland. My whole world opened up when I realized that I can, indeed, be friends with people who differ from me. What a gift this was! I have beloved friends who disagree with me on gender roles, politics, religion—some of the issues dearest to me, of which I think, *How could you not see it this way?* But they don't, and I love them, not from a distance but really and truly.

If a chapter on faith is going to completely ruin this book for you, then don't read it. But I am going to ask you to consider hearing me out because, like everything else in here, this is for our kids.

Faith is the best gift we can give our children. A nice childhood is one thing, but to know you are loved by the One who made you is an unwavering, ever-present comfort that carries you all of your days.

As a teenager I was lying in bed trying to fall asleep when I was tortured by a solitary thought. Eventually it swelled up inside and I had no choice. I did what I had always done as a little girl—I crept down the stairs and knocked on my mom's door. (Dad was away on business, which made it feel less awkward.)

I made up some excuse for not being able to sleep and crept into the other side of the king-sized bed. I waited a few minutes to make my question feel more natural and unprompted. "Mom?" I said into the darkness. "Do you ever wonder if all the stuff in the Bible isn't true?" I held my breath under the comforter. It felt really important that she answer this well.

"Well," she said, with kindness, thoughtfulness, and not a smidgen of overreaction. "I've always thought of it this way: even if it's all untrue, my life is infinitely better by living God's way." I was so relieved I nearly cried.

1. Mom had thought this too.
2. Her answer made sense.
3. I had the freedom to think.

I am not afraid of my children's questions. I hope they ask them. And I hope I answer with the grace and love my mother did.

The second reason I include this chapter is for us, the parents. To me, it is a deep comfort to know that my children ultimately are not in my hands. I will fail miserably at times doing all the things I have talked about in this book, and so will you. Even if we did everything perfectly, there are no guarantees. But this is not the end of the story *because it is not up to us*. I can't say it any better than one of my favorite authors, Paul David Tripp, in his book, *Parenting*:

> Your success as a parent does not rest on your shoulders but on his. . . . He would never ever think of sending us out on our own. He would never coldly watch us at a distance as we go, work, and struggle. He would never sit idly by as we give ourselves to the single hardest, most comprehensive, most long-term, most exhausting, and most life-shaping task that a human being could ever take on. No, when your Father sends you, he goes with you. This means that in every moment when you are parenting, you are being parented. . . . In every moment when you feel alone, you are anything but alone because he goes wherever you go. . . . He never forgets you, he never turns his back on you, he never wanders away for a moment, he never favors someone else over you, he never gets mad and refuses to be with you, he never grows cynical, he will never give up, and he will never ever quit. . . . So your hope as a parent is not found in your power, your wisdom, your character, or your success, but in this one thing alone: the presence of your Lord.[1]

Jesus has been so faithful to me, all of my days—the most in the darkest times. The times that should have been the scariest and worst are precious to me because he was there. I want my children to know this Jesus. To know him even a smidgen keeps alive the hope that his ways are best. In the pages to come I will talk specifically about being the kind of parent that my mom was to me in the darkness: one not afraid of questions about faith, who lives authentically, and who passes on hope.

When Your Kids Are Just Really Naughty
but You Love Them Anyway

Yesterday after church, an older woman came up to me with the sweetest smile. "Your kids are *so* well behaved. You can tell they know exactly what's expected of them, and you hold a high standard, and they rise up to it."

I turned around to see if she was talking to someone else. She wasn't. And then I laughed. Boy, do we have these people fooled! Somehow they missed my hushed commands through gritted teeth and the fight I broke up during the Apostle's Creed and me sopping up the unauthorized cup of pre-church juice that spilled under the seats.

And, truthfully, none of these incidents were all that naughty. What she *really* should witness is some of the end-of-day tantrums. Maybe she'd sing a different tune.

In *Loving the Little Years*, Rachel Jankovic notes,

> This is not a tender reminiscence from someone who had children so long ago that she only remembers the sweet parts. I don't have a foggy, precious perspective on mothering little ones. . . . At the time of writing this, I have three children in diapers, and I can recognize the sound of hundreds of toothpicks being dumped out in the hall.[2]

This is how I feel about writing a chapter on naughty kids. As I type these words, I can still smell the Peace and Calming essential oil I rubbed on my wrists this morning after a messy altercation involving a fight, a vacuum cleaner, and a baby doll. I'm still trying to de-stress my breathing from the tension of putting a child in time-out who did not want to go in time-out. The last time I was in the bathroom, come to think of it, was to sit in a quiet room on a blue Rubbermaid step stool and pray that God would save all of us who live here from ourselves.

Unfortunately I have no ten-step, secret-sauce guarantee to crank out kids who grow up to be church elders, Eagle Scouts, or Christian character award winners or, at the very least, people who don't end up in jail at some point. (If you know someone who sells this secret sauce, order me at least a box.) But what I can do is offer suggestions, things I have done while attempting, like you, to raise godly human beings.

- **Expect much.**

  No matter what the circumstances, there should be absolute nonnegotiables that are expected in your home. Period. I tend to make up excuses for my kids. To not punish the stomping up the stairs because "she's really tired." To avoid a consequence because I yelled, too, and Mommy shouldn't have yelled. And sometimes, I wonder if there's "something else big" going on that is making my kid act like a demon-possessed rage-monster. I tend to jump to worst-case potential scenarios. This means that when my kids do something totally horrid, my mind runs through all kinds of scenarios, like *what if they have some sort of mental illness or disorder or something?* Because you never know, right? At one point during one child's irrational outburst, I voiced this concern to my mom, who wisely said, "Even if there were something wrong, *even if*—some things just aren't tolerated in your house. You have to make that clear."

  I thought about that a bit. It's true. We already have our hard-and-fast standards in other arenas. My kids know, for example, that they're always going to wear their seat belts. They understand after years of repetition that no matter how sick or angry or uncomfortable they are, the seat belt is a nonnegotiable. So what has happened in the behavioral realm, I've realized, is that I have let some things become negotiable that are actually nonnegotiable. Things such as *We don't throw things. We don't hit people. We don't say "I hate you."* Just to name a few. So I had to perform a tricky parental operation known as Back the Bus Up. I say, "Sorry, kids, I've been doing this wrong. We do not allow this (whatever it is) in our home."

I found it interesting that I'm not the only mom who makes up excuses for kids being naughty. In *The Collapse of Parenting*, Leonard Sax notes,

> I regularly encounter parents . . . who wonder whether their child might have rapid-cycling bipolar disorder or some other neuropsychiatric explanation for bad behavior. I explain to those parents that it's normal for an eight-year-old to swing through different moods in half an hour. Sometimes in just five minutes. . . . I say it over and over again: The job of the parent is to teach self-control. To explain what is and is not acceptable. To establish boundaries and enforce consequences.[3]

I don't know where you need to Back the Bus Up. I don't know what's going on in your house that has become negotiable that should go back to nonnegotiable. It's hard to tell sometimes. Praying is helpful as is imagining that *someone else's* kid did what your kid is doing. Would you think, *Wow. That kid should not be allowed to do that!?* That's probably a good point to take action.

• **Don't be afraid to discipline.**

Oh, this is the hardest most awful part for many of us. I struggle to think up consequences, but have eventually realized you have to "hit them where it hurts," figuratively speaking. So many parents are afraid to actually take away privileges. Try to think about the extras that mean the most; it will vary from age to stage to child. It might be fruit snacks. It might be *PAW Patrol* or going to a party or dessert or a late bedtime or an iPad or playing with friends. Hit them where it hurts. And note that oftentimes it will hurt *you* more than it will hurt them. You will be the one breaking up fights instead of relaxing while they watch a show. You will be the one entertaining them and listening to tantrums while they don't play with friends. *Be strong*, though. It's a good fight.

- **Use stories.**

    You can share stories about your own childhood, your friend's childhood, your husband's. Sometimes I make up stories, too, and I think this is 100 percent okay. Like this. "I know this boy who throws these really big tantrums, and his mom and dad don't punish him. I really hope that he gets better because if he grows up and does something bad when he's angry, the police could come, and he could go to jail!" There are about a thousand oversimplifications in there, but I'm sharing a story of what could happen when someone lives with uncontrolled anger. I also tell stories from my own life. I'll say, "One time I was really angry, and I threw my cell phone. It's not okay in our house. Dad told me I could never do that again." (Unfortunately this story is in the nonfiction category. Are you noticing a trend here? We struggle with losing our tempers.)

- **Have a sense of humor.**

    One time I saw my neighbor outside on her front porch, swaying back and forth on the rocking chair, reading a magazine, drinking lemonade. She waved a cheery hello. "Hey! Oh, I'm just sitting out here because my kids are all screaming and being really naughty while they're in time-out." (another big smile and laugh) "Oh well! I'll enjoy the sunshine." Contrast this to yours truly, who tends to text her husband and say things like "This is the worst day ever, and I can't stop crying and please come home right away because I can't listen to these kids anymore okay please and thank you."

What my neighbor was exhibiting is the ability to detach yourself in a healthy way from your kids' behavior. I need to learn this lesson quickly because teenager-hood is less than three years away. I love my kids deeply, and it is my primary job to raise them to glorify God, but their ultimate choices are theirs, not mine. Deep breath. "You want to do crazy nonsensical things like crawl across the floor while moaning and whining? Fine! That's your poor choice! Oh well, I'll get back to my phone conversation."

- **Pay attention to meeting their needs.**

I'm weird, but one of my pet peeves is seeing kids out after their bedtimes. The other night my husband and I were downtown at nearly ten o'clock in the evening. We walked through the city streets to see two kids screaming bloody murder. One was being dragged along the sidewalk and the other carried, and neither was in pajamas. Now, certainly there could have been some reasonable explanation. Maybe they were on their way to urgent care because someone had suddenly spiked a fever. Or maybe their uncle was just arriving from Afghanistan on an airplane and they were greeting him after a four-year absence. I mean, who knows. In any case, those kids were not behaving very well, but they had a good excuse. They were exhausted and wanted to be sleeping.

It's easier for me to see this in other families than to see it happening in my own. I'm just too close to the trees to see the forest. I have realized that I expect everyone else to give *me* grace when I'm struggling, but I'm not great at giving grace to my kids when they struggle. I'm trying to get better, but I'm not naturally in tune to others' needs (sigh). Unmet needs do not excuse awful behavior, but it is kind to understand if there is an underlying need. Is someone grumpy because they are hungry? Thirsty? Need a nap? Introverted and have seen enough people? Sad about losing that last game of Candy Land? Worried about a test tomorrow? Getting sick? Meet the need and then address the misbehavior. Often it will clear up anyway.

- **Remind them they belong.**

Verbally remind them often that "you are one of us." This is more important during sticky and stressful moments. Sometimes when I'm addressing a behavior that I'm basically shocked has ever made it into our home, I will say, "This is not okay. You are a Smartt. We don't do that. Smartts don't act like that." Instead of it being an isolating moment that makes someone feel like they're just plain naughty and awful, it is (I hope) a moment that draws them back into the fold and calls them to a higher standard. That is the key to it. Communicate that "family is forever. I will never leave you. We are in this for the long haul, you and I. There is nothing you can do to lose my love."

One evening I was licking my wounds after a particularly exhausting day of parenting. I don't mean the kind of exhausting like "Wow, we walked twenty miles at Disneyland today! What a day. I'm gonna sleep well!" No. This was the kind of exhaustion that accompanies the deep doubt of everything. Your calling, your methods, your abilities, your belief that these children are going to make it out of childhood all right. That exhaustion hovered over me that night at the computer, and somehow I stumbled upon the beautiful song "In the Morning," by J. J. Heller. It was the grace that I needed and my kids needed. I cried at the first line: "It's been a long day, and you did your best." I encourage you to listen to this song on your next discouraging day of parenting. How blessed we are that his mercies are always fresh in the morning and that we can begin again tomorrow.

Live What You Say

For my first real job I was the librarian at a Christian school. (I hear you out there making your librarian jokes.) We had to arrive at 7:15 a.m. for morning devotions, led by the pastor of the church. Interesting plot twist: ten years later that same pastor pled guilty to stealing nearly $1 million from the church and school. I still remember a lot of what he said at devotions. Do you think that I esteem those words now? No. I don't. Rightly or not, for me, he has lost all credibility; he was inauthentic in his character, and I don't trust him.

I wonder if the relational equivalent of this is happening in the houses of well-intentioned Christian families. I wonder if there is a chasm between action and word, between character and doctrine. I wonder if what we say does not seem to mean anything.

You might think this observation is unrelated to all the previous chapters, but precisely the opposite is true. *Simply put, are we a family who, together, lives this Good Life?*

If I tell my kids to get their rear ends off the couch and have adventures, am I myself moving my own rear end toward adventures?

If I tell my kids that too much technology is harmful, am I myself stuck scrolling my phone?

If I tell my kids that being cool doesn't matter, am I chasing the latest iPhone, applying gobs of concealer before I leave the house, or ordering new clothes every three weeks from this or that boutique?

If I tell them to be kind, am I myself screaming at their dad when I get mad?

If I tell them reading matters, when was the last time I picked up a book?

If I tell them faces are more important than screens, do I look them in the eyes when they're talking to me?

If you are like me, this list of questions surfaces a little bit of a guilty, depressed feeling. We have high ideals, and yet we are very, very human. People sometimes take this to mean we drop the ideals. Embrace the imperfect, stop trying so hard. I get the appeal of this, but it essentially falls flat and is unhelpful.

My pastor sometimes tells us he wants to be the "first repenter." I think this sums up a better response to the guilty, depressed feeling. In this response we don't stop trying. We confess first.

Part of the good news about being a parent is that you have a built-in accountability system! Isn't that wonderful? A friend of mine said he told his daughters they could ask for five dollars every time they saw him using his phone while driving. Don't you bet that habit was broken quickly!

I'm going to be honest with you. There's something scary about writing a parenting book when your kids are all ten and under. I don't use words like *jinx*, but if I did, I might feel like using it here. The jury is very much still out. I don't have a proven formula. But, honestly, I'm not sure you should believe me if I said I did. What I do have is this: Work out your faith with fear and trembling in front of your kids. Be authentic but give them truth. I can't resist quoting Paul David Tripp again:

> If we are going to teach our children to run to Jesus daily, we must run to Jesus daily as well. If we want our children to be sad in the face of the sin of their hearts and hands, we must mourn our sin as parents as well. You see, it is only as we are willing to confess that we are more like than unlike our children, that we ourselves need parenting every day, that we will be parents in need of a father's grace who will again and again lead our children to the grace of the Father.[4]

I think this is one of the most exciting parts of this whole thing. We all learn together. Together, we adventure. Together, we choose faces over screens. Together, we apologize and pick ourselves up again tomorrow. Together, we chase after the Good Life.

FAMILY MISSION STATEMENT

Just as it is important to know who you are as an individual, it's important to know who you are as a family. These principles can help guide your thoughts and actions.

We believe in adventure, embracing lives of wonder and joy. We believe in intentionality, in filling our time with things that matter—and sometimes that's nothing. We believe in community, that real life is found with others. We believe in presence, in using technology as a tool to live well. We believe in stewardship, in using our stuff and money well. We believe in wisdom, enjoying media and books that make our lives richer. We believe in work, that there's nothing like a job well done. We believe in integrity, that it's okay to be different if it means you do the right thing. We believe in kindness and that friendship is one of God's greatest gifts. We believe in respect, in treating others the way we would want to be treated. We believe in service and that the best way out of a funk is to help someone else. We believe in family and that we will always have one another's backs. We believe in grace because we are forgiven, and we can forgive. We believe in purity and that real joy comes from obeying God. We believe in faith and that eternity matters most.

RESOURCES

Books to Read with Your Kids
Before They Leave Home

Young Children

Frog and Toad, by Arnold Lobel

Horton Hears a Who, by Dr. Seuss

The Jesus Storybook Bible, by Sally Lloyd-Jones

Just in Case You Ever Wonder, by Max Lucado

Little Bear series, by Else Holmelund Minarik

Mike Mulligan and His Steam Shovel, by Virginia Lee
Burton

The Velveteen Rabbit, by Margery Williams

Winnie-the-Pooh, by A. A. Milne (also good for elementary-
aged children)

You Are Special, by Max Lucado

Elementary-Aged Children

The Hundred Dresses, by Eleanor Estes

20,000 Leagues Under the Sea, by Jules Verne

The Boxcar Children, (and others) by Gertrude Chandler Warner

Caddie Woodlawn, by Carol Ryrie Brink

Calvin and Hobbes comics, by Bill Watterson

Charlie and the Chocolate Factory, by Roald Dahl

Charlotte's Web, by E. B. White

Chronicles of Narnia series, by C. S. Lewis

Farmer Boy, (and others) by Laura Ingalls Wilder

Garfield comics, by Jim Davis

The Green Ember series, by S. D. Smith

Heidi, by Johanna Spyri

The Last of the Really Great Whangdoodles, by Julie Andrews Edwards

Missionary biographies (We love the Christian Heroes Then and Now series, by Janet and Geoff Benge.)

One Wintry Night, by Ruth Bell Graham

The Secret Garden, by Frances Hodgson Burnett

The Shining Sword, by Charles G. Coleman

Stuart Little, by E. B. White

The Trailblazer Series, by Dave and Neta Jackson

Trumpet of the Swan, by E. B. White

Where the Red Fern Grows, by Wilson Rawls

A Wrinkle in Time, by Madeleine L'Engle

Older Children

The Adventures of Huckleberry Finn, by Mark Twain

Anne of Green Gables, by L. M. Montgomery

Born Again, by Charles W. Colson

The Fellowship of the Ring, by J. R. R. Tolkien

God's Smuggler, by Brother Andrew (also good for elementary)

The Hiding Place, by Corrie ten Boom

RESOURCES

Little Women and *Little Men*, by Louisa May Alcott
Number the Stars, by Lois Lowry
Pollyanna, by Eleanor H. Porter
To Kill a Mockingbird, by Harper Lee
The Wind in the Willows, by Kenneth Grahame
Wingfeather Saga, by Andrew Peterson
Wonder, by R. J. Palacio

Movies to Watch As a Family Before Your Kids Leave Home

Disclaimer: Kids and families differ in their tastes and preferences. Your kids may or may not be ready for the intensity in some of these movies, so always make decisions based on what is best for your particular kids.

Movies Appropriate for the Whole Family

101 Dalmatians, 1961
Akeelah and the Bee
Anne of Green Gables
Annie
The Aristocats
Babe
Bambi
Beauty and the Beast, 1991
Ben-Hur
Black Beauty
Brave Little Toaster
Charlotte's Web
Cheaper by the Dozen, 1949
Chronicles of Narnia movies
Cinderella, 1950
Christmas cartoons
DuckTales the Movie
Facing the Giants
The Fox and the Hound
Gifted Hands
Harvey, 1950
Heidi
Herbie movies

Homeward Bound 1 and 2
Hugo
The Jungle Book
Inside Out
It's a Wonderful Life
Lady and the Tramp
The Little Rascals
Mary Poppins, 1964
Mr. Magorium's Wonder Emporium
Mr. Smith Goes to Washington
My Fair Lady
Newsies
Night at the Museum
Oklahoma
Paddington II
The Peanuts Movie
The Perfect Game
Pollyanna
The Princess Bride
Ratatouille
Remember the Titans
Robin Hood, 1973
Seven Brides for Seven Brothers
Shirley Temple movies, *The Little Princess* especially
The Sound of Music
The Swiss Family Robinson
The Ten Commandments
Toy Story
White Christmas
Winnie the Pooh
The Wizard of Oz

Movies to Enjoy (for Age-Appropriate
Children) with Adult Supervision
   (**Note:** research content and choose when these would be
      appropriate for your family's viewing.)
   Amazing Grace
   Angels in the Outfield
   The Avengers movies
   Chariots of Fire
   Cool Runnings
   Davy Crockett movies
   End of the Spear
   The Hiding Place
   Hook
   I Can Only Imagine
   Iron Will
   The Lord of the Rings trilogy
   The Man from Snowy River 1 and 2
   The Passion of the Christ
   Paul, Apostle of Christ
   Pride and Prejudice
   The Pursuit of Happyness
   Rudy
   Sense and Sensibility
   Star Wars movies
   Twelve Angry Men
   What About Bob?
   Wonder

Conversations to Have with Your Kids Before They Leave Home

Instructions: Use these questions as starting points for discussions about important things. My hope is that these will stir up good conversations—not just that you would ask the questions and listen but that you would use the time as an opportunity to share your own beliefs with your children.

On Friendship

- Have you ever heard someone making fun of someone else? What did you do?
- Has someone ever told you something that wasn't true? How did you feel?
- Is it wrong to say something bad about someone if they're not around to hear it?
- Can you remember something nice someone said to you? Can you remember something mean someone said to you?
- Do you ever feel different from other kids? Do you think it's okay to be different?
- What makes a good friend? How can you be a good friend, and how can you find a good friend?
- What does it mean to have good manners?

On Family

- Do you think boys and girls act differently? What is Mom good at and what is Dad good at?
- Is there anything you could do that would make Mom or Dad stop loving you?
- What makes our family special?
- What is the purpose of sex, and who should be able to have sex? (Obviously this important topic is for kids who are mature enough to handle this conversation.)

On Ethics

- What should you do if you find something that doesn't belong to you? What do you think of the phrase "finders keepers"?
- Have you ever been tempted to steal something? Do you think stealing is ever okay?
- Do you think anything is really hidden or secret?
- Have you ever told a lie? What is the best thing to do if you have told a lie?
- Why is it important to do a good job in the small things in life, such as making your bed or doing your best on a paper?
- Which matters more: winning or doing the right thing?
- Who decides what makes something wrong or right?
- Why should we be kind to people who won't ever really be able to "pay us back"?
- Is it wrong to be lazy? Why or why not?

On Dreams

- Can money make you happy?
- What should you do if you need help making a decision?
- Do you think there is one person you are meant to marry?
- What are you good at? What are gifts that God has given to you?
- What qualities make a good husband or wife? Is it good looks, being popular, being funny? Or something else?
- Do you ever wish God had made you differently? Do you wish you looked different or had different traits or abilities?

On Faith

- Does God always answer prayers?
- Is heaven a real place? How do you get there?
- Is there anyone who has never done anything wrong?
- What do you think you should do if you feel guilty about something?

On Personal Choices

- What do you think makes good hygiene?
- What do you do if you're worried about something or afraid of something?
- Can you think of something scary you saw on TV that got stuck in your head? Why is it important to be careful what you put in your head?
- Which is more fun: watching TV or playing outside?

On Family History

- Tell each child his or her birth story.
- Tell the story of how you and your husband met.
- Tell your kids about a mistake you made and what you learned from that mistake.
- Tell your kids about each of your grandparents if you're able: their personalities, where they lived, their jobs, and a memory you have with them.

Things Children Should
Always Have on Hand

- age-appropriate Bible
- baby doll
- baseball glove and ball, basketball and hoop, and soccer ball. (We have an indoor basketball hoop over-the-door version that has been replaced twice because it is so well loved.) Also someone to play these games with!
- books on their reading level
- creative-play, open-ended building toys (LEGOs, blocks, interlocking cubes, train tracks, Magna-Tiles)
- drawing and coloring materials: crayons, colored pencils, paper, and so on
- good music
- helmet, a bike, and a place to ride
- library card
- opportunity to dig in the dirt
- pocket knife (around age seven or older)
- puzzles
- running shoes
- sensory play items, such as Play-Doh and tools
- sewing basket or other handiwork
- stuffed-toy friend

Best Family Games

Younger Children
    Candy Land
    Chutes and Ladders
    Connect Four
    Hide-and-Go-Seek
    Hopscotch
    Hoot Owl Hoot
    I Spy
    Kick the Can
    Race to the Treasure
    Sequence for Kids
    The Sneaky, Snacky Squirrel Game
    Sorry
    Sum Swamp
    Trouble

Older Children
    Apples to Apples
    Battleship
    Blokus
    Capture the Flag
    Catan
    Checkers
    Chess
    Chicken Dominoes
    Clue
    Codenames
    Exploding Kittens
    Four Square

Hearts
Kemps
Kickball
Life
Mastermind
Monopoly
Pictionary
Quiddler
Quixx
Qwirkle
Risk
Rummy
Scrabble
Spaces
Stratego
Ticket to Ride
Ultimate Frisbee
UNO

ACKNOWLEDGMENTS

So often in the process of creating this book, I felt overwhelmed and unqualified. I asked God for help and he answered. Thank you, Lord, for this good work to do and the strength to do it.

To Todd: You lifted my head when I was discouraged, washed the dishes when I was exhausted, prayed for me, believed in me, and didn't even read the book until it was printed. Such confidence! You're my favorite.

To Sam, Ty, and Ellie: If I could pick any three kids to be mine, I would pick you. Being your mother is my greatest gift.

Mom and Dad: You model the Good Life so well. Thank you for the sacrifices you made so that we could be kids and for the sacrifices you make now so that our kids can be kids.

To my sisters, my biggest cheerleaders and best friends: thank you for praying, editing, brainstorming, babysitting, and cheerleading.

John: Who would have guessed I'd end up coming to you for advice on all sorts of things. I adore the man you've become.

To my *bonus* sisters, Morgan, Julianne, and Helen: Each of you is such a treasure. I love raising our little ones together!

To my brothers-in-law: Because of you, my kids will grow up with lots of great uncle stories (which is really important). How dull would life be, really, without you all annoying me?

To Carole and Doug: You do many things well—community, marriage, and laughter. My children are blessed to have you, and so am I.

To Ashley, Emily, and Catherine: my faithful, sweet prayer warriors. I am grateful for you!

To Katie: thank you for watching seven loud kids while I wrote in a quiet Starbucks, for processing the ideas in this book, and for reminding me that what I was doing mattered.

To Bill Jensen: I would have given up on this project long ago without your unfailing wisdom, encouragement, and humor. You've championed this message on every level. I am beyond grateful for you.

To Debbie: We did it! Can you believe it? Thank you for always being so gracious, good-humored, and for getting the vision.

To Natalie: This book is so much better because of you. Thank you for being so kind and gracious when you pointed out all my mistakes!

To Katherine, Paula, and the W team: Your wonderful partnership is an overwhelming gift. I am beyond honored to work with you.

To the many, many friends and family members who asked how my writing was coming, shared the book, and acted excited when I was done: Thank you! If I tried to list all of your names, I would surely leave someone out, but know that I noticed every kindness and am so very grateful!

To my Christian mastermind author friends who have prayed, counseled, and encouraged through every step of my writing journey: you all are the best.

ACKNOWLEDGMENTS

Thank you, finally, to those who generously offered their stories and words of wisdom to the process of writing this book: Carole Smartt, Cliff Wright, Jessica James, Jessica Gray, Karen Toney, Chip Sneed, Sid Druin, Karin Drescher, Hudson Belk, Sheila Carlberg, and Melanie Hempe.

NOTES

Chapter 1: Why Childhood Matters

1. Rachel Hosie, "Is It Impossible to Change Your Personality After 30?" Independent, June 14, 2017, https://www.independent.co.uk /life-style/personality-change-past-age-30-is-it-possible-psychology -kirsten-godfrey-david-buss-carol-rothwell-a7757866.html.

2. Leonard Sax, *The Collapse of Parenting* (New York: Basic Books, 2016), 122–23. Dr. Sax notes several studies that say self-control in children continues to be maintained throughout adulthood and, furthermore, is the single greatest indicator of adult success and wealth.

3. "Unraveling How Kids Become Bilingual So Easily," Associated Press, July 20,2009, http://ilabs.washington.edu/news/MSNBC _UW_I-LABS.pdf. This article claims that the ability to learn language (your own or another) markedly declines after puberty.

4. "Evangelism Is Most Effective Among Kids," Barna, October 11, 2004, https://www.barna.com/research/evangelism-is-most -effective-among-kids/. This Barna study indicated that two-thirds of Christians profess Christ before their twenty-first birthday.

5. Ben Sassy, *The Vanishing American Adult* (New York: St. Martin's Press, 2017), 106.

6. Cindy Rollins, *Mere Motherhood: Morning Times, Nursery Rhymes, and My Journey Toward Sanctification* (Concord, NC: CiRCE Institute, 2016), 131.

7. Kristi Clover, "Tricia Goyer: When God Uses Your Pain & Your Past for Good in Your Life," *Simply Joyful Podcast*, January 27, 2017, https://kristiclover.com/sjp-002-tricia-goyer-god-uses-pain-past-good-life.

Chapter 2: The Gift of Adventure

1. Kim Brooks, "We Have Ruined Childhood," *New York Times*, August 17, 2019, https://www.nytimes.com/2019/08/17/opinion/sunday/childhood-suicide-depression-anxiety.html.
2. Monica Swanson, *Boy Mom* (Colorado Springs: Waterbrook, 2019), 34.
3. Richard Louv, *Last Child in the Woods* (Chapel Hill, NC: Algonquin Books, 2008), 100.
4. Louv, *Last Child*, 109.
5. Louv, 10.
6. Kim John Payne, *Simplicity Parenting: Using the Extraordinary Power of Less to Raise Calmer, Happier, and More Secure Kids* (New York: Ballantine Books, 2010), 98.

Chapter 3: The Gift of Boredom

1. Most of this essay is derived from my blog post "How (and Why) to Give Your Kids an 80's Childhood (Step One: Let Them Get Real Bored)," *"Smartter" Each Day*, http://smarttereachday.com/give-kids-80s-childhood-step-1-let-get-real-bored/.
2. Tim Vernimmen, "Where Creativity Comes From," *Scientific American*, September 16, 2016, https://www.scientificamerican.com/article/where-creativity-comes-from. This article explains that humans (and most animals) need to feel safe to innovate or create.
3. Kim Brooks, "We Have Ruined Childhood," *New York Times*, August 17, 2019, https://www.nytimes.com/2019/08/17/opinion/sunday/childhood-suicide-depression-anxiety.html.
4. Karin Drescher, personal interview, October 12, 2019.
5. For an extensive look at the benefits of nature in child development, I recommend *Last Child in the Woods*, by Richard Louv.

Chapter 4: The Gift of Being Uncool

1. A 2019 Common Sense Media study reported that children between the ages of eight and twelve spend four to five hours a day on screens, and that teenagers spend over seven hours on screens (not counting time for school). Study cited in Rachel Siegel, "Tweens, Teens and Screens: The Average Time Kids Spend Watching Online Videos Has Doubled in 4 Years," *Washington Post*, October 29, 2019, https://www.washingtonpost.com /technology/2019/10/29/survey-average-time-young-people-spend -watching-videos-mostly-youtube-has-doubled-since.

2. Ben Sasse, *The Vanishing American Adult: Our Coming-of-Age Crisis—and How to Rebuild a Culture of Self-Reliance* (New York: St. Martin's Press, 2017), 98.

3. Parts of this essay are from my blog post "Reinstate the Awkward Years," *"Smartter" Each Day*, http://smarttereachday.com/give-kids -80s-childhood-step-2-reinstate-awkward-years.

4. Jessica Gray, personal interview, October 29, 2019.

5. I tell the entire story of Samule the Mule in my blog post "The Velveteen Samule," *"Smartter" Each Day*, http://smarttereachday .com/the-velveeteen-samule.

Chapter 5: The Gift of Imagination

1. There are many online articles that validate the role of play in child development. Here is one: Alison Gopnik, "Let the Children Play, It's Good for Them!," *Smithsonian*, July 2012, https://www .smithsonianmag.com/science-nature/let-the-children-play-its -good-for-them-130697324. In addition, see Stuart Brown, *Play* (New York: Penguin, 2010).

2. Carole Smartt, personal interview, October 17, 2019.

3. Jessica James, personal interview, October 21, 2019.

4. Perri Klass, "Reading Aloud to Young Children Has Benefits for Behavior and Attention," *New York Times*, April 16, 2018, https:// www.nytimes.com/2018/04/16/well/family/reading-aloud-to -young-children-has-benefits-for-behavior-and-attention.html.

5. Jessica Smartt, "The iPhone Is Ruining Your Summer," HuffPost, July 27, 2015, https://www.huffpost.com/entry/screen-time -unplugging_b_7881152.
6. Study cited in Ben Sasse, *The Vanishing American Adult: Our Coming-of-Age Crisis—and How to Rebuild a Culture of Self-Reliance* (New York: St. Martin's Press, 2017), 39.
7. Melanie Hempe, "Families Managing Media" (lecture, NorthCross Church, Cornelius, NC, February 1, 2019).
8. Hempe, "Families Managing Media."
9. Chip Sneed, personal interview, June 19, 2017.
10. I realize that getting kids unaddicted from technology is akin to delivering a baby with no medication: epically painful, requiring much willpower, and not to be attempted alone. For practical help on freeing your kids from addictive screens, I recommend the resources on Screen Strong (www.screenstrong.com).

Chapter 6: The Gift of Balance

1. Jessica Gray, personal interview, October 29, 2019.
2. Hudson Belk, personal interview, July 26, 2019.
3. Leonard Sax, *The Collapse of Parenting: How We Hurt Our Kids When We Treat Them Like Grown-Ups* (New York: Basic Books, 2016), 99.
4. Karen Toney, personal interview, November 29, 2019.
5. I am indebted to Karen Toney for her thoughts on how to let kids fail well.

Chapter 7: The Gift of Grit

1. Ben Sasse, *The Vanishing American Adult: Our Coming-of-Age Crisis—and How to Rebuild a Culture of Self-Reliance* (New York: St. Martin's Press, 2017), 122.
2. Cal Newport, *Deep Work: Rules for Focused Success in a Distracted World* (New York: Grand Central Publishing, 2018).
3. Sasse, *Vanishing American Adult*, 210.
4. Leonard Sax, *The Collapse of Parenting: How We Hurt Our Kids*

When We Treat Them Like Grown-Ups (New York: Basic Books, 2016), 122–23.

Chapter 8: The Gift of Manners and Kindness

1. Marcie Bianco, "Ellen DeGeneres and George W. Bush Cowboys Meet-Up Reveals the Cost of Acceptance," NBC News, October 8, 2019, https://www.nbcnews.com/think/opinion /ellen-degeneres-george-w-bush-s-cowboys-pal-around-reveals -ncna1064181.
2. To select a child for your family to sponsor, visit Compassion.com.

Chapter 9: The Gift of Family

1. Cliff Wright, personal interview, February 18, 2019.
2. Gordon Neufeld and Gabor Mate, MD, *Hold On to Your Kids: Why Parents Need to Matter More Than Peers* (New York: Ballantine Books, 2006), 7.
3. Leonard Sax, *The Collapse of Parenting: How We Hurt Our Kids When We Treat Them Like Grown-Ups* (New York: Basic Books, 2016), 104–105.
4. Rachel Jankovic, *Loving the Little Years* (Moscow, ID: Canon Press, 2010), 79.
5. Susan Schaeffer Macaulay, *For the Children's Sake* (Wheaton, IL: Crossway Books, 1984), 23.

Chapter 10: The Gift of Innocence

1. Carole Smartt, personal interview, October 17, 2019.
2. Leonard Sax, *The Collapse of Parenting: How We Hurt Our Kids When We Treat Them Like Grown-Ups* (New York: Basic Books, 2016), 7–8.
3. Kim John Payne, *Simplicity Parenting: Using the Extraordinary Power of Less to Raise Calmer, Happier, and More Secure Kids* (New York: Ballantine Books, 2010), 163.
4. Payne, *Simplicity Parenting*, 189.
5. Payne, 189–190.

6. Melanie Hempe, "Families Managing Media" (lecture, NorthCross Church, Cornelius, NC, February 1, 2019).

7. Kristin MacLaughlin, "The Detrimental Effects of Pornography on Small Children," Net Nanny, December 19, 2017, https://www .netnanny.com/blog/the-detrimental-effects-of-pornography-on -small-children/.

8. Kristen A. Jenson, *Good Pictures Bad Pictures: Porn-Proofing Today's Young Kids* (Richland, WA: Glen Cove Press, 2017).

9. Sarah Hinstorff, "Escape Tricky Situations with a Code Word," Center for Parent & Teen Communication, September 4, 2018, https://parentandteen.com/tips-for-teens-escape-situations-with-a -code-word.

10. Hempe, "Families Managing Media."

Chapter 11: The Gift of Faith

1. Paul David Tripp, *Parenting: The 14 Gospel Principles That Can Radically Change Your Family* (Wheaton, IL: Crossway, 2016), 187–188.

2. Rachel Jankovic, *Loving the Little Years* (Moscow, ID: Canon Press, 2010), 12.

3. Leonard Sax, *The Collapse of Parenting: How We Hurt Our Kids When We Treat Them Like Grown-Ups* (New York: Basic Books, 2016), 50.

4. Tripp, *Parenting*, 56–57.

ABOUT THE AUTHOR

Jessica Smartt is a former English teacher turned homeschooling mama of three. A week after her first baby was born, she began her motherhood blog, *"Smartter" Each Day*. Jessica and her husband live in beautiful North Carolina, where she loves hiking with kids (mostly), steaming coffee in the afternoon, family bike rides, and anything that's ever been done to a potato.

It's Never Too Late to Become a Memory-Making Mom

What's the secret to the rich, meaningful life that you're longing to have with your family?
Create traditions that bring both joy and purpose.

In *Memory-Making Mom*, author Jessica Smartt highlights ten tradition-gifts that children need most and includes a rich resource of two hundred–plus unique traditions.

No matter where you are or what your family looks like, you can begin today to create more adventure, more celebrations, and more meaning. Make lasting memories and breathe new life into your home.

AVAILABLE IN PRINT, E-BOOK, AND AUDIO

To learn more about Jessica, visit
smarttereachday.com

and stay in touch on Facebook and Instagram:
@jessica.smartt

9 780785 221272